the hummingbird bakery
cookbook

the hummingbird bakery
cookbook

Tarek Malouf and The Hummingbird Bakers

photography by Peter Cassidy
and Kate Whitaker

Mitchell Beazley

An Hachette UK Company
www.hachette.co.uk

First published in Great Britain in 2009 by
Ryland Peters & Small
This revised and expanded edition published in 2017
by Mitchell Beazley, a division of
Octopus Publishing Group Ltd
Carmelite House, 50 Victoria Embankment
London EC4Y 0DZ
www.octopusbooks.co.uk

Text, layouts and 2009 photography © Tarek
Malouf and The Hummingbird Bakery 2009, 2017
2017 photography © Octopus Publishing Group 2017

ISBN 978-1-78472-416-0
A CIP catalogue record for this book is available
from the British Library.
Printed and bound in China
10 9 8 7 6 5 4 3 2 1

Notes
• For the recipes on pages 14–53 and 132–143,
please use standard muffin cases.
• All spoon measurements are level, unless
otherwise specified.
• All eggs are large, unless otherwise specified. It is
generally recommended that free-range eggs
be used. Uncooked or partially cooked eggs should
not be served to the very young, the very old,
those with compromised immune systems, or
to pregnant women.
• Ovens should be preheated to the specified
temperature.
• Where recipes require white vinegar, use distilled
white vinegar, white wine vinegar or cider vinegar.

**For useful baking tips from
The Hummingbird Bakery, go to:**
hummingbirdbakery.com

For the 2009 edition:
**Design, Photographic Art Direction
and Prop Styling** Steve Painter
Senior Editor Céline Hughes
Production Manager Patricia Harrington
Art Director Leslie Harrington
Publishing Director Alison Starling

Photographer Peter Cassidy
Food Stylist Bridget Sargeson

Hummingbird Bakery corporate branding
and company graphic design Sue Thedens
Illustrations Debbie Adamson

For this edition:
Publisher Alison Starling
Art Director Juliette Norsworthy
Junior Editor Ella Parsons
Senior Production Manager Katherine Hockley
Production Controller Dasha Miller

Photographer (including front cover image) Kate Whitaker
Food Styling Annie Rigg
Prop Styling Olivia Wardle

contents

Welcome to The Hummingbird Bakery

I first thought about opening The Hummingbird Bakery after spending Thanksgiving with my cousins in North Carolina. After eating too much pie, I wondered why there wasn't somewhere in London that made these types of traditional American desserts that I had grown up eating.

I started planning the Bakery in 2002. It's hard to imagine now, but back then cupcakes were almost unknown in the UK, and American baking in general wasn't highly regarded. First I attended baking classes in New York, so that I would understand the ingredients and techniques used in traditional American baking. Then came the fun task of devising recipes, and testing them on friends and family, making me incredibly popular! I always had an idea of which cakes and bakes I wanted to sell, and for these I tested and tweaked many recipes until I found what I thought tasted the most authentic.

Luckily a unit in Portobello Road, in London's Notting Hill, soon came up by chance and I immediately jumped on it. It proved to be heaven-sent because, as soon as the shop opened, a lot of high-profile customers began to write and speak about us. People soon began queuing up to try our cupcakes and other goodies.

After all these years, we still sell more cupcakes than any other single product, with Red Velvet being the all-time favourite and best-seller. As time went by, however, our layer cakes started to catch up and today, I feel that we are known for our authentic American desserts, and not just for cupcakes, and that is something I'm very proud of.

As the baking boom began to grow, thanks in part to *The Hummingbird Bakery Cookbook*, ingredients and equipment became much more readily available in the UK. With that in mind, and using the valuable feedback from our millions of readers worldwide, I decided it was time to revisit some of the recipes and incorporate some of the tricks and tips the Hummingbird bakers and I have gathered since the first edition was published in 2009!

The biggest change has been in the cupcake section: as large American-style muffin cases have become the norm, we've been able to increase the yield of the recipes so that the size of the cupcakes match the size we sell in our shops. New variants of food colourings and baking ingredients also mean that the home baker has more choice and we've tried to adapt the recipes to match this trend.

Finally, a tip that we've given out many times: every oven is unique, baking slow or fast, so please invest in an oven thermometer and remember, the cooking times are just a guide, a cake is only done when it's done!

I'm so pleased to be able to continue to share my favourite traditional American cakes and bakes with you in this new edition. I hope you enjoy baking them as much as we all have over the years at The Hummingbird Bakery.

Tarek Malouf

frostings

These frostings make enough to frost one batch of cupcakes, or one cake. They are used in cupcake and cake recipes throughout the book. Dye the vanilla frosting any shade you like with a couple of drops of food colouring mixed in until evenly incorporated – remember, start with a very few drops to avoid overly dark colours that will stain tongues! At The Hummingbird Bakery, we like our cupcake frostings in pretty candy colours, but you can choose any colour you like.

vanilla

500 g icing sugar, sifted
160 g unsalted butter, at room temperature
50 ml whole milk
½ teaspoon vanilla extract

Makes enough to frost 16 cupcakes or one 20-cm cake

Beat the icing sugar and butter together in a freestanding electric mixer with a paddle attachment (or use a handheld electric whisk) on medium-slow speed until the mixture comes together and is well mixed. It will have a sandy texture. Turn the mixer down to slow speed. Combine the milk and vanilla extract in a separate bowl, then add to the butter mixture a couple of spoonfuls at a time. Once all the milk has been incorporated, turn the mixer up to high speed. Continue beating until the frosting is light and fluffy, at least five minutes. The longer the frosting is beaten, the fluffier and lighter it becomes.

chocolate

450 g icing sugar, sifted
150 g unsalted butter, at room temperature
120 g cocoa powder, sifted
120 ml whole milk

Makes enough to frost 16 cupcakes or one 20-cm cake

Beat the icing sugar, butter and cocoa powder together in a freestanding electric mixer with a paddle attachment (or use a handheld electric whisk) on medium-slow speed until the mixture comes together and is well mixed. It will have a sandy texture. Turn the mixer down to slow speed. Add the milk to the butter mixture a couple of spoonfuls at a time. Once all the milk has been incorporated, turn the mixer up to high speed. Continue beating until the frosting is light and fluffy, at least five minutes. The longer the frosting is beaten, the fluffier and lighter it becomes.

cream cheese

600 g icing sugar, sifted
100 g unsalted butter, at room temperature
250 g cream cheese, cold

Makes enough to frost 16 cupcakes or one 20-cm cake

Beat the icing sugar and butter together in a freestanding electric mixer with a paddle attachment (or use a handheld electric whisk) on medium-slow speed until the mixture comes together and is well mixed. It will have a sandy texture. Add the cream cheese in one go and beat until it is completely incorporated. Turn the mixer up to medium-high speed. Continue beating until the frosting is light and fluffy, at least five minutes. Do not overbeat, as it can quickly become runny.

cupcakes

vanilla cupcakes

Our vanilla cupcakes, topped with candy-coloured vanilla frosting and sprinkles, are what first made The Hummingbird Bakery famous, and they still never fail to please. The batter is runny, so don't worry, and don't overcook them – they should be light golden and spring back when touched. Try topping them with chocolate frosting as well. To make a three-layer, 20-cm cake, double the quantities and bake in three, 20-cm sandwich tins.

240 g plain flour

280 g caster sugar

3 teaspoons baking powder

¼ teaspoon salt

80 g unsalted butter,
at room temperature

240 ml whole milk

2 eggs

½ teaspoon vanilla extract

1 quantity Vanilla Frosting (page 11)

hundreds and thousands, or other edible sprinkles, to decorate

*two 12-hole cupcake trays,
lined with 16 paper cases
(see note on page 4)*

Makes 16

Preheat the oven to 175°C (160°C fan)/Gas 4.

Put the flour, sugar, baking powder, salt and butter in a freestanding electric mixer with a paddle attachment (or use a handheld electric whisk) and beat on slow speed until you get a sandy consistency and everything is combined. Gradually pour in half the milk and beat until the milk is just incorporated.

Whisk the eggs, vanilla extract and remaining milk together in a separate bowl for a few seconds, then pour into the flour mixture and continue beating until just incorporated (scrape any unmixed ingredients from the side of the bowl with a rubber spatula). Continue mixing for a couple more minutes until the mixture is smooth. Do not overmix.

Spoon the mixture into the paper cases until one-third full and bake in the preheated oven for 18–20 minutes, or until light golden and the sponge bounces back when touched. A skewer inserted in the centre should come out clean. Leave the cupcakes to cool for about 15 minutes in the trays before turning out onto a wire cooling rack to cool completely.

When the cupcakes are cold, spoon the Vanilla Frosting onto each cupcake, gently smoothing over with a palette knife and making a swirl of frosting on each one. Decorate with hundreds and thousands.

chocolate cupcakes

We use a devil's food cake recipe for our chocolate base. The cocoa powder gives the sponge a dark colour and chocolatey kick. The sponge should be light and moist, with all the ingredients well incorporated. But don't overbeat the mixture, or the sponge will be too heavy. For chocolate lovers, top with Chocolate Frosting. For a more restrained option, both the Vanilla and Cream Cheese Frostings work well.

200 g plain flour

40 g cocoa powder

280 g caster sugar

3 teaspoons baking powder

¼ teaspoon salt

80 g unsalted butter,
at room temperature

240 ml whole milk

2 eggs

½ teaspoon vanilla extract

1 quantity Chocolate, Vanilla or Cream Cheese Frosting (page 11)

chocolate vermicelli or edible silver balls, to decorate

*two 12-hole cupcake trays,
lined with 16 paper cases
(see note on page 4)*

Makes 16

Preheat the oven to 175°C (160°C fan)/Gas 4.

Put the flour, cocoa powder, sugar, baking powder, salt and butter in a freestanding electric mixer with a paddle attachment (or use a handheld electric whisk) and beat on slow speed until you get a sandy consistency and everything is combined.

Whisk the milk, eggs and vanilla extract together in a jug, then slowly pour about half into the flour mixture, beat to combine and turn the mixer up to high speed to get rid of any lumps.

Turn the mixer down to a slower speed and slowly pour in the remaining milk mixture (scrape any unmixed ingredients from the side of the bowl with a rubber spatula). Continue mixing for a couple more minutes until the mixture is smooth. Do not overmix.

Spoon the mixture into the paper cases until one-third full and bake in the preheated oven for 20–25 minutes, or until the sponge bounces back when touched. A skewer inserted in the centre should come out clean. Leave the cupcakes to cool for about 15 minutes in the trays before turning out onto a wire cooling rack to cool completely.

When the cupcakes are cold, spoon the Chocolate, Vanilla or Cream Cheese Frosting onto each cupcake, gently smoothing over with a palette knife and making a swirl of frosting on each one. Decorate with chocolate vermicelli or silver balls.

red velvet cupcakes

It seems people can't resist our Red Velvet cupcakes. Mix all the ingredients well so that the sponge has an even colour and texture. For added colour contrast, crumble some extra red velvet sponge over the cupcakes. To make a red velvet cake instead, double the quantities below, divide between three 20-cm cake tins and bake for 25 minutes at the same oven temperature.

120 g unsalted butter, at room temperature

300 g caster sugar

2 eggs

20 g cocoa powder

1 tablespoon red food colouring paste, such as Sugarflair 'Red Extra', mixed with 3 tablespoons water

1 teaspoon vanilla extract

240 ml buttermilk

300 g plain flour

1 teaspoon salt

1 teaspoon bicarbonate of soda

3 teaspoons white vinegar

1 quantity Cream Cheese Frosting (page 11)

two 12-hole cupcake trays, lined with 16 paper cases (see note on page 4)

Makes 16

Preheat the oven to 175°C (160°C fan)/Gas 4.

Put the butter and the sugar in a freestanding electric mixer with a paddle attachment (or use a handheld electric whisk) and beat on medium speed until light and fluffy and well mixed. Turn the mixer up to high speed, slowly add the eggs and beat until everything is well incorporated.

In a separate bowl, mix together the cocoa powder, red food colouring and vanilla extract to make a thick, dark paste. Add to the butter mixture and mix thoroughly until evenly combined and coloured (scrape any unmixed ingredients from the side of the bowl with a rubber spatula). Turn the mixer down to slow speed and slowly pour in half the buttermilk. Beat until well mixed, then add half the flour, and beat until everything is well incorporated. Repeat this process until all the buttermilk and flour have been added. Scrape down the side of the bowl again. Turn the mixer up to high speed and beat until you have a smooth, even mixture. Turn the mixer down to low speed and add the salt, bicarbonate of soda and vinegar. Beat until well mixed, then turn up the speed again and beat for a couple more minutes.

Spoon the mixture into the paper cases until one-third full and bake in the preheated oven for 20–25 minutes, or until the sponge bounces back when touched. A skewer inserted in the centre should come out clean. Leave the cupcakes to cool for about 15 minutes in the trays before turning out onto a wire cooling rack to cool completely.

When the cupcakes are cold, spoon the Cream Cheese Frosting onto each cupcake, gently smoothing over with a palette knife and making a swirl of frosting on each one.

lemon cupcakes

Lemon is always a popular alternative to chocolate or vanilla desserts. The trick is to keep the frosting slightly tart, to temper the sugar.

240 g plain flour

300 g caster sugar

3 teaspoons baking powder

2 tablespoons finely grated lemon zest, plus extra to decorate

80 g unsalted butter, at room temperature

240 ml whole milk

2 eggs

lemon frosting

500 g icing sugar, sifted

160 g unsalted butter, at room temperature

4 tablespoons finely grated lemon zest

a couple of drops of yellow food colouring (optional)

50 ml whole milk

two 12-hole cupcake trays, lined with 16 paper cases (see note on page 4)

Makes 16

Preheat the oven to 175°C (160°C fan)/Gas 4.

Put the flour, sugar, baking powder, lemon zest and butter in a freestanding electric mixer with a paddle attachment (or use a handheld electric whisk) and beat on slow speed until you get a sandy consistency and everything is combined. Gradually pour in the milk and beat until just incorporated.

Add the eggs to the flour mixture and continue beating until just incorporated (scrape any unmixed ingredients from the side of the bowl with a rubber spatula). Continue mixing for a couple more minutes until the mixture is smooth. Do not overmix.

Spoon the mixture into the paper cases until one-third to half full and bake in the preheated oven for 20–25 minutes, or until the sponge bounces back when touched. A skewer inserted in the centre should come out clean. Leave the cupcakes to cool for about 15 minutes in the trays before turning out onto a wire cooling rack to cool completely.

For the lemon frosting: Beat together the icing sugar, butter, lemon zest and food colouring, if using, in a freestanding electric mixer with a paddle attachment (or use a handheld electric whisk) on medium-slow speed until the mixture comes together and is well mixed. Turn the mixer down to a slower speed. Slowly pour in the milk, then when it is all incorporated, turn the mixer up to high speed. Continue beating until the frosting is light and fluffy, at least five minutes. The longer the frosting is beaten, the lighter and fluffier it becomes.

When the cupcakes are cold, spoon the lemon frosting onto each cupcake, gently smoothing over with a palette knife and making a swirl of frosting on each one, and decorate with a little lemon zest.

almond and raspberry cupcakes

These cupcakes have a different sort of sponge, made with almond milk instead of cow's milk. We've decorated with almond flakes that have been lightly toasted for flavour and colour.

300 g plain flour

2½ teaspoons baking powder

1 teaspoon bicarbonate of soda

½ teaspoon salt

300 g caster sugar

100 g ground almonds

270 ml almond milk

125 ml vegetable oil

¼ teaspoon almond extract

200 g raspberry jam

25 g flaked almonds, to decorate (optional)

mascarpone frosting

500 g mascarpone cheese

350 g icing sugar, sifted

½ teaspoon vanilla extract

75 g raspberries, crushed with the back of a spoon

two 12-hole deep muffin trays, lined with 16 paper cases (see note on page 4)

Makes 16

Preheat the oven to 175°C (160°C fan)/Gas 4.

Sift the flour, baking powder, bicarbonate of soda and salt into a freestanding electric mixer with a paddle attachment (or use a handheld electric whisk), add the sugar and ground almonds and beat on slow speed until well incorporated.

Put the almond milk, oil and almond extract in a jug and whisk to combine. Slowly pour into the flour mixture and beat until all the ingredients are just incorporated. Turn the mixer up to medium speed and continue beating for a couple more minutes until the mixture is smooth and well combined.

Spoon the mixture into the paper cases until about one-third full and bake in the preheated oven for 18–20 minutes until the sponge bounces back when touched. A skewer inserted into the centre should come out clean. Leave the cupcakes to cool for about 15 minutes in the trays before turning out onto a wire cooling rack to cool completely.

For the mascarpone frosting: Beat together the mascarpone, icing sugar and vanilla extract in a freestanding electric mixer with a whisk attachment (or use a handheld electric whisk) on a slow speed until the sugar is incorporated. Turn the mixer up to medium speed and beat until the frosting is well combined and smooth. Stir in the crushed raspberries by hand until just incorporated.

When the cupcakes are cold, use a sharp knife to hollow out a small section in the centre of each cake, approximately 2 cm in diameter and 3 cm deep. Keep the sponge pieces. Spoon (or pipe) the raspberry jam into the hollows, then top with the sponge pieces. If you have any jam left over, spread it thinly over the top of each cake, making sure not to go over the edges. Spoon the frosting onto each cupcake, gently smoothing over with a palette knife and making a swirl of frosting on each one. Decorate with flaked almonds, if using.

strawberry cheesecake cupcakes

It's important to use pieces of fresh strawberry in this recipe – they moisten the sponge and improve the texture of the cupcakes. The fruit will sink whilst baking and settle towards the bottom in a sort of gooey compote, this is normal. The crumbled digestive biscuits sprinkled on top add the flavour of a cheesecake base.

240 g plain flour

280 g caster sugar

3 teaspoons baking powder

¼ teaspoon salt

80 g unsalted butter,
at room temperature

240 ml whole milk

1 teaspoon vanilla extract

2 eggs

16 large strawberries, chopped into small pieces

25–50 g digestive biscuits

1 quantity Cream Cheese Frosting (page 11)

two 12-hole cupcake trays, lined with 16 paper cases (see note on page 4)

Makes 16

Preheat the oven to 175°C (160°C fan)/Gas 4.

Put the flour, sugar, baking powder, salt and butter in a freestanding electric mixer with a paddle attachment (or use a handheld electric whisk) and beat on slow speed until you get a sandy consistency and everything is combined.

Pour in the milk and vanilla extract and beat on medium speed until all the ingredients are well mixed (scrape any unmixed ingredients from the side of the bowl with a rubber spatula). Add the eggs and beat well for a few minutes to ensure the ingredients are well incorporated.

Divide the chopped strawberries between the paper cases. Spoon the cupcake mixture on top until two-thirds full and bake in the preheated oven for 20–25 minutes, or until light golden and the sponge bounces back when touched. A skewer inserted in the centre should come out clean. Leave the cupcakes to cool for about 15 minutes in the trays before turning out onto a wire cooling rack to cool completely.

Roughly break up the digestive biscuits and put them in a food processor. Process until finely ground. When the cupcakes are cold, spoon the Cream Cheese Frosting onto each cupcake, gently smoothing over with a palette knife and making a swirl of frosting on each one. Finish with a sprinkling of finely ground biscuits.

sticky fig and pistachio cupcakes

Figs, honey and pistachio give these cupcakes a slightly Middle Eastern twist. Roughly chop the pistachios for decoration, sprinkling them around a dollop of fig jam.

80 ml vegetable oil

3 tablespoons runny honey

220 g caster sugar

2 large eggs

3 tablespoons strong black coffee or espresso, cooled slightly

½ teaspoon vanilla extract

230 g plain flour

¼ teaspoon salt

¼ teaspoon ground cinnamon

1 tablespoon baking powder

200 g fig jam, plus extra to decorate

50 g crushed pistachio nuts, to decorate

honey frosting

210 g unsalted butter, at room temperature

350 g icing sugar, sifted

½ teaspoon vanilla extract

2 tablespoons double cream

2 tablespoons runny honey

140 g mascarpone cheese

two 12-hole deep muffin trays, lined with 16 paper cases (see note on page 4)

Makes 16

Preheat the oven to 175°C (160°C fan)/Gas 4.

Put the oil, honey, sugar, eggs, coffee and vanilla extract in a freestanding electric mixer with a paddle attachment (or use a handheld electric whisk) and beat on a medium speed until all the ingredients are well combined.

In a separate bowl, mix together the flour, salt, cinnamon and baking powder, then slowly add to the egg mixture, continuing to beat until everything is smooth and well mixed.

Spoon the mixture into the paper cases until about one-third full and bake in the preheated oven for 18–20 minutes until the sponge bounces back when touched. A skewer inserted into the centre should come out clean. Leave the cupcakes to cool for about 15 minutes in the trays before turning out onto a wire cooling rack to cool completely.

For the honey frosting: Beat the butter in a freestanding electric mixer with a paddle attachment (or use a handheld electric whisk) on medium speed for a few minutes to loosen, then add the icing sugar, vanilla extract, cream and honey and continue beating for two to three minutes until light and fluffy. Add the mascarpone and beat until the frosting is smooth and well combined.

When the cupcakes are cold, use a sharp knife to hollow out a small section in the centre of each cake, approximately 2 cm in diameter and 3 cm deep. Keep the sponge pieces. Spoon the fig jam into a piping bag and pipe into the hollows, then top with the sponge pieces.

Spoon the frosting onto each cupcake, gently smoothing over with a palette knife and making a swirl of frosting on each one. Decorate with the crushed pistachios and a small dollop of fig jam, which you can pipe or spoon on.

black bottom cupcakes

The black bottom cupcake looks innocent, but packs a punch! A dark chocolate sponge with a dollop of cheesecake baked into it, we top ours with Cream Cheese Frosting and a sprinkling of cocoa powder for extra impact. The chocolate sponge base is different from our normal chocolate cupcakes – it's darker and firmer, slightly less sweet and marries well with the cheesecake. Omit the cream cheese frosting for a more moderate treat.

1 quantity Cream Cheese Frosting
(page 11) (optional)

chocolate sponge

270 g plain flour

285 g caster sugar

55 g cocoa powder,
plus extra to decorate

1¼ teaspoons bicarbonate of soda

100 ml sunflower oil

1½ teaspoons white vinegar

1½ teaspoons vanilla extract

200 ml water

cheesecake filling

185 g cream cheese

110 g caster sugar

1 egg

1 teaspoon vanilla extract

a pinch of salt

100 g milk chocolate chips

*two 12-hole cupcake trays,
lined with 16 paper cases
(see note on page 4)*

Makes 16

Preheat the oven to 175°C (160°C fan)/Gas 4.

For the chocolate sponge base: Put the flour, sugar, cocoa powder and bicarbonate of soda in a large bowl and mix with a handheld electric whisk on slow speed until well mixed.

Put the oil, vinegar, vanilla extract and water in a jug and whisk to combine. While the electric whisk is running in the flour bowl, slowly add the contents of the jug, increasing the speed of the blender as the mixture thickens. Continue to beat until all the ingredients are incorporated (scrape any unmixed ingredients from the side of the bowl with a rubber spatula).

Spoon the mixture into the paper cases until one-third full and set aside.

For the cheesecake filling: Beat together the cream cheese, sugar, egg, vanilla extract and salt in a freestanding electric mixer with a paddle attachment (or use a handheld electric whisk) on medium-slow speed until smooth and fluffy.

Stir in the chocolate chips by hand until evenly dispersed. Don't overmix, otherwise the cream cheese will start to split.

Scoop about 1 tablespoon of the cheesecake filling onto the cupcake mixture in the cases and bake in the preheated oven for about 20 minutes, or until the cupcakes are firm to the touch and there is an even golden colour on the cheesecake filling. Don't overcook as the cheesecake will become very dry and crumbly. Leave the cupcakes to cool for about 15 minutes in the trays before turning out onto a wire cooling rack to cool completely.

When the cupcakes are cold, spoon the Cream Cheese Frosting, if using, on top, gently smoothing over with a palette knife. Decorate with a light sprinkling of cocoa powder.

lavender cupcakes

Many people can't imagine eating a lavender-flavoured cake, but this is a very popular flavour in the summer. Infusing the milk with lavender flowers, which you can buy online, makes the floral taste subtle. The icing can be left plain, or you can use a bit of food colouring to give it a light lavender colour.

240 ml whole milk

6 tablespoons dried lavender flowers

240 g plain flour

280 g caster sugar

3 teaspoons baking powder

80 g unsalted butter,
at room temperature

2 eggs

16 small sprigs of lavender,
to decorate (optional)

lavender frosting

50 ml whole milk

2 tablespoons dried lavender flowers

500 g icing sugar, sifted

160 g unsalted butter,
at room temperature

a couple of drops of purple food
colouring (optional)

*two 12-hole cupcake trays,
lined with 16 paper cases
(see note on page 4)*

Makes 16

Put the milk and dried lavender flowers in a jug, cover and refrigerate for a few hours, or overnight if possible. Repeat with the milk and lavender flowers for the frosting, in a separate jug.

Preheat the oven to 175°C (160°C fan)/Gas 4.

Put the flour, sugar, baking powder and butter in a freestanding electric mixer with a paddle attachment (or use a handheld electric whisk) and beat on slow speed until you get a sandy consistency and everything is combined.

Strain the lavender-infused milk (for the cupcakes) and slowly pour into the flour mixture, beating well until all the ingredients are well mixed. Add the eggs and beat well (scrape any unmixed ingredients from the side of the bowl with a rubber spatula).

Spoon the mixture into the paper cases until one-third full and bake in the preheated oven for 20–25 minutes, or until the sponge bounces back when touched. A skewer inserted in the centre should come out clean. Leave the cupcakes to cool for about 15 minutes in the trays before turning out onto a wire cooling rack to cool completely.

For the lavender frosting: Beat together the icing sugar, butter and food colouring, if using, in a freestanding electric mixer with a paddle attachment (or use a handheld electric whisk) on medium-slow speed until the mixture comes together and is well mixed. Turn the mixer down to slow speed. Strain the lavender-infused milk and slowly pour into the butter mixture. Once all the milk is incorporated, turn the mixer up to high speed. Continue beating until the frosting is light and fluffy, at least 5 minutes. The longer the frosting is beaten, the fluffier and lighter it becomes.

When the cupcakes are cold, spoon the lavender frosting onto each cupcake, gently smoothing over with a palette knife and making a swirl of frosting on each one. Decorate with a sprig of lavender, if using.

hazelnut and chocolate cupcakes

Sometimes chocolate alone just won't do, which is why we've added irresistible hazelnut chocolate spread to these cupcakes. Decorate with hazelnuts for extra crunch.

200 g plain flour

40 g cocoa powder

280 g caster sugar

3 teaspoons baking powder

¼ teaspoon salt

80 g unsalted butter, at room temperature

240 ml whole milk

2 eggs

180 g hazelnut and chocolate spread (such as Nutella) softened

about 48 whole, shelled hazelnuts, to decorate

hazelnut and chocolate frosting

500 g icing sugar, sifted

160 g unsalted butter, at room temperature

50 ml whole milk

160 g hazelnut and chocolate spread (such as Nutella)

two 12-hole cupcake trays, lined with 16 paper cases (see note on page 4)

Makes 16

Preheat the oven to 175°C (160°C fan)/Gas 4.

Put the flour, cocoa powder, sugar, baking powder, salt and butter in a freestanding electric mixer with a paddle attachment (or use a handheld electric whisk) and beat on slow speed until you get a sandy consistency and everything is combined.

Slowly pour the milk into the flour mixture, beating well well mixed. Add the eggs and beat well (scrape any unmixed ingredients from the side of the bowl with a rubber spatula).

Spoon the mixture into the paper cases until two-thirds full and bake in the preheated oven for about 20 minutes, or until the sponge bounces back when touched. Leave the cupcakes to cool for about 15 minutes in the trays before turning out onto a wire cooling rack to cool completely.

When the cupcakes are cold, use a sharp knife to hollow out a small section in the centre of each cake, approximately 2 cm in diameter and 3 cm deep. Keep the sponge pieces. Fill each cupcake with a dollop of hazelnut and chocolate spread. Warmed spoons will help to do this (I dipped teaspoons in a jug of hot water). Top with the sponge pieces.

For the hazelnut and chocolate frosting: Beat the icing sugar and butter together in a freestanding electric mixer with a paddle attachment (or use a handheld electric whisk) on medium-slow speed until the mixture comes together and is well mixed. The mixture will have a sandy texture. Turn the mixer down to a slower speed. Slowly pour in the milk, then when it is all incorporated, turn the mixer up to high speed. Continue beating until the frosting is light and fluffy, at least five minutes. The longer the frosting is beaten, the fluffier and lighter it becomes.

Stir in the hazelnut and chocolate spread by hand until evenly mixed. Spoon the frosting onto each cupcake, gently smoothing over with a palette knife and making a swirl of frosting on each one. Finish with about three hazelnuts per cupcake.

hot cross bun cupcakes

With spices that you'd find in a Hot Cross Bun, you may end up making these all year round!

125 g caster sugar

100 g soft light brown sugar

finely grated zest of ½ orange

2 large eggs

100 g natural yogurt

25 ml orange juice

100 ml sunflower oil

200 g plain flour

2 teaspoons baking powder

1 teaspoon mixed spice

1 teaspoon ground cinnamon

¼ teaspoon ground ginger

¼ teaspoon ground nutmeg

¼ teaspoon ground cloves

75 g sultanas

50 g mixed peel

1 small Granny Smith apple, peeled, cored and chopped into 1-cm cubes

cross decorations

100 g white chocolate, roughly chopped

2 tablespoons double cream

cinnamon frosting

100 g unsalted butter, at room temperature

600 g icing sugar, sifted

250 g cream cheese, cold

1¼ teaspoons ground cinnamon, plus extra to decorate (optional)

two 12-hole deep muffin trays, lined with 16 paper cases (see note on page 4)

Makes 16

For the decorations: Put the chocolate and cream in a heatproof bowl over a saucepan of simmering water (do not let the base of the bowl touch the water). Leave until melted and smooth, stirring occasionally until completely combined. Remove from the heat and leave to cool and thicken.

Using a marker pen, mark out 16 crosses, each 4 x 4 cm, on a piece of baking parchment, then flip the sheet over and place on a baking tray. Spoon the chocolate mixture into a piping bag fitted with a size 12 nozzle. Using the marked-out crosses as a guide, pipe on the chocolate mixture to form the decorations. Leave to set for three to four hours in a cool place, or overnight if possible.

Preheat the oven to 175°C (160°C fan)/Gas 4.

Put both sugars, the orange zest, eggs, yogurt, orange juice and oil in a freestanding electric mixer with a paddle attachment (or use a handheld electric whisk) and beat on medium speed until well incorporated. Sift the flour, baking powder and spices into a separate bowl. Turn the mixer down to slow speed, then slowly add the flour mixture to the egg mixture, beating until incorporated. Be careful not to overmix.

Fold the sultanas, mixed peel and apple cubes into the mixture by hand until evenly dispersed.

Spoon the mixture into the paper cases until about one-third full and bake in the preheated oven for 18–20 minutes until the sponge bounces back when touched. A skewer inserted into the centre should come out clean. Leave the cupcakes to cool for about 15 minutes in the trays before turning out onto a wire cooling rack to cool completely.

For the cinnamon frosting: Beat the butter in a freestanding electric mixer with a paddle attachment (or use a handheld electric whisk) on medium speed for a few minutes to loosen. Turn the mixer down to slow speed and add the icing sugar in three stages until it is well incorporated, then turn the mixer up to medium speed and beat for five minutes. Add the cream cheese and cinnamon in one go and beat until completely incorporated. Turn the mixer up to high speed and continue beating for another two to three minutes until the frosting is light and fluffy. Do not overbeat, as it can quickly become runny.

Spoon the frosting onto each cupcake, gently smoothing over with a palette knife until the frosting is flat and smooth. Top with the cross decorations and sprinkle with cinnamon, if using.

coconut and pineapple cupcakes

Coconut and pineapple give these cupcakes a tropical flavour. As with any sponge that has moist fruit added to it, the fruit may sink towards the bottom of the cupcake as it bakes, this is normal. Grated, fresh coconut can be used instead of desiccated coconut for an even better taste.

240 g plain flour

280 g caster sugar

3 teaspoons baking powder

¼ teaspoon salt

80 g unsalted butter,
at room temperature

240 ml coconut milk

1 teaspoon vanilla extract

2 eggs

350 g tinned pineapple rings (drained weight), chopped into small pieces

desiccated coconut, to decorate

coconut frosting

500 g icing sugar, sifted

160 g unsalted butter,
at room temperature

50 ml coconut milk

25 g dessicated coconut

*two 12-hole cupcake trays,
lined with 16 paper cases
(see note on page 4)*

Makes 16

Preheat the oven to 175°C (160°C fan)/Gas 4.

Put the flour, sugar, baking powder, salt and butter in a freestanding electric mixer with a paddle attachment (or use a handheld electric whisk) and beat on slow speed until you get a sandy consistency and everything is combined.

Mix the coconut milk and vanilla extract in a separate bowl, then beat into the flour mixture on medium speed until well combined. Add the eggs and beat well (scrape any unmixed ingredients from the side of the bowl with a rubber spatula).

Divide the chopped pineapple between the paper cases. Spoon the cupcake mixture on top until two-thirds full and bake in the preheated oven for 20–25 minutes, or until light golden and the sponge bounces back when touched. A skewer inserted in the centre should come out clean. Leave the cupcakes to cool for about 15 minutes in the trays before turning out onto a wire cooling rack to cool completely.

For the coconut frosting: Beat the icing sugar and butter together in a freestanding electric mixer with a paddle attachment (or use a handheld electric whisk) on medium-slow speed until the mixture comes together and is well mixed. Turn the mixer down to a slower speed and slowly pour in the coconut milk. Once all the milk has been incorporated, turn the mixer up to high speed. Continue beating until the frosting is very white, light and fluffy, five to ten minutes.

When the cupcakes are cold, spoon the coconut frosting onto each cupcake, gently smoothing over with a palette knife and making a swirl of frosting on each one. Finish with a sprinkling of desiccated coconut.

banana and chocolate cupcakes

Bananas work so well when used in baking, as they become almost caramel-like as they cook. The smoother you mash your bananas, the more incorporated they will be into the sponge. Chocolate Frosting works particularly well with these, but Vanilla or Cream Cheese Frosting can also be used.

240 g plain flour

280 g caster sugar

3 tablespoons baking powder

2 teaspoons ground cinnamon

2 teaspoons ground ginger

¼ teaspoon salt

160 g unsalted butter,
at room temperature

175 ml whole milk

2 eggs

200 g peeled banana, mashed

1 quantity Chocolate Frosting
(page 11)

20 g dark chocolate, grated with
a cheese grater into shavings

*two 12-hole cupcake trays,
lined with 16 paper cases
(see note on page 4)*

Makes 16

Preheat the oven to 175°C (160°C fan)/Gas 4.

Put the flour, sugar, baking powder, cinnamon, ginger, salt and butter in a freestanding electric mixer with a paddle attachment (or use a handheld electric whisk) and beat on slow speed until you get a sandy consistency and everything is combined.

Slowly pour the milk into the flour mixture, beating well until all the ingredients are well mixed. Add the eggs and beat well (scrape any unmixed ingredients from the side of the bowl with a rubber spatula).

Stir in the mashed banana by hand until evenly dispersed.

Spoon the mixture into the paper cases until one-third full and bake in the preheated oven for about 20 minutes, or until light golden and the sponge bounces back when touched. Leave the cupcakes to cool for about 15 minutes in the trays before turning out onto a wire cooling rack to cool completely.

When the cupcakes are cold, spoon the Chocolate Frosting onto each cupcake, gently smoothing over with a palette knife and making a swirl of frosting on each one. Finish with the chocolate shavings.

cranachan cupcakes

A cupcake that we serve for St Andrew's Day, bringing together a trio of Scottish flavours: oats, raspberries and whisky.

50 g rolled oats

240 g plain flour

280 g caster sugar

1 tablespoon baking powder

¼ teaspoon salt

80 g unsalted butter, at room temperature

240 ml whole milk

2 large eggs

3 tablespoons whisky

cream filling

200 ml double cream

2 teaspoons icing sugar

65 g raspberries, roughly chopped, plus 16 extra raspberries, to decorate (optional)

whisky and honey frosting

340 g unsalted butter, at room temperature

375 g icing sugar, sifted

60 ml whisky

60 ml double cream, plus extra if needed

1 teaspoon runny honey

1 teaspoon vanilla extract

two 12-hole deep muffin trays, lined with 16 paper cases (see note on page 4)

Makes 16

Preheat the oven to 150°C (130° fan)/Gas 2. Put the rolled oats on a baking tray and toast in the oven for 6–10 minutes until golden. Be careful not to burn them. Leave to cool.

Turn the oven up to 175°C (160°C fan)/Gas 4.

Put the flour, sugar, baking powder, salt and butter in a freestanding electric mixer with a paddle attachment (or use a handheld electric whisk) and beat on slow speed until you get a sandy consistency and everything is well combined.

Slowly pour half the milk into the flour mixture, beating on a medium-slow speed until it is just incorporated. Whisk the eggs into the remaining milk, then pour into the flour mixture and continue beating until just incorporated (scrape any unmixed ingredients from the side of the bowl with a rubber spatula). The mixture will be quite runny. Stir in the toasted oats by hand.

Spoon the mixture into the paper cases until about one-third full and bake in the preheated oven for 18–20 minutes until the sponge bounces back when touched. A skewer inserted into the centre should come out clean.

When the hot cupcakes come out of the oven, pour a small amount of whisky over each one. Leave to soak and cool for about 15 minutes in the trays before turning out onto a wire cooling rack to cool completely.

For the cream filling: Put the cream and icing sugar in a freestanding electric mixer with a whisk attachment (or use a handheld electric whisk) and beat until the cream thickens into whipped cream. Be careful not to over-whisk otherwise the cream will split. Stir in the raspberries by hand until they are evenly dispersed. Set aside.

For the whisky and honey frosting: Beat the butter in a freestanding electric mixer with a paddle attachment (or use a handheld electric whisk) on medium speed for a few minutes to loosen. Turn the mixer down to slow speed and add the icing sugar in three stages until it is well incorporated. Turn up to high speed and continue to beat for two to three minutes. Turn the mixer down to a slower speed and slowly pour in the whisky, double cream, honey and vanilla extract until incorporated, then continue to mix on medium speed for a couple more minutes until the frosting is light and fluffy. If the frosting is too stiff, add 1 teaspoon of cream at a time until you reach a good consistency.

When the cupcakes are cold, use a sharp knife to hollow out a small section in the centre of each cake, approximately 2 cm in diameter and 3 cm deep. Keep the sponge pieces. Spoon the cream filling into a piping bag and pipe into the hollows, then top with the sponge pieces. If you have any filling left over, spread it thinly over the top of each cake, making sure not to go over the edges.

Spoon the frosting onto each cupcake, gently smoothing over with a palette knife and making a swirl of frosting on each one. Decorate each with a raspberry, if using.

green tea cupcakes

Green tea-flavoured desserts are very popular in Japan. It's a flavour that works so well in cakes, combined with either vanilla or chocolate. It's important to use green tea powder called 'matcha'. Buy it online or from tea shops and specialist Asian supermarkets.

240 ml whole milk

6 matcha green tea bags

200 g plain flour

40 g cocoa powder

280 g caster sugar

3 teaspoons baking powder

¼ teaspoon salt

80 g unsalted butter,
at room temperature

2 eggs

½ teaspoon vanilla extract

green tea frosting

500 g icing sugar, sifted

160 g unsalted butter,
at room temperature

40 g matcha green tea powder,
plus extra to decorate

50 ml whole milk

*two 12-hole cupcake trays,
lined with 16 paper cases
(see note on page 4)*

Makes 16

Put the milk and green tea bags in a jug, cover and refrigerate for a few hours, or overnight if possible.

Preheat the oven to 175°C (160°C fan)/Gas 4.

Put the flour, cocoa powder, sugar, baking powder, salt and butter in a freestanding electric mixer with a paddle attachment (or use a handheld electric whisk) and beat on slow speed until you get a sandy consistency and everything is combined.

Remove the green tea bags from the infused milk and combine with the eggs and vanilla extract. Slowly pour half into the flour mixture, beating well until the ingredients are well mixed. Turn the mixer up to high speed and beat well to ensure there are no lumps. Turn the speed down to medium-slow and slowly pour in the remaining milk mixture (scrape any unmixed ingredients from the side of the bowl with a rubber spatula). Continue mixing for a couple more minutes until the mixture is smooth.

Spoon the mixture into the paper cases until one-third full and bake in the preheated oven for 20–25 minutes, or until the sponge bounces back when touched. A skewer inserted in the centre should come out clean. Leave the cupcakes to cool for about 15 minutes in the trays before turning out onto a wire cooling rack to cool completely.

For the green tea frosting: Beat together the icing sugar, butter and matcha powder in a freestanding electric mixer with a paddle attachment (or use a handheld electric whisk) on medium-slow speed until the mixture is well mixed. Turn the mixer down to a slower speed. Slowly pour in the milk, then when it is all incorporated, turn the mixer up to high speed. Continue beating until the frosting is light and fluffy, at least five minutes.

When the cupcakes are cold, spoon the frosting on top, gently smoothing over with a palette knife and making a swirl of frosting on each one. Decorate with a light sprinkling of matcha powder.

peaches and cream cupcakes

A classic summer combination, using fresh peaches makes the recipe work so much better. The peaches will release their moisture as they cook and tend to sink towards the bottom, so don't worry. Other fruits in season could be substituted.

240 g plain flour

280 g caster sugar

3 teaspoons baking powder

¼ teaspoon salt

80 g unsalted butter,
at room temperature

240 ml whole milk

2 eggs

½ teaspoon vanilla extract

300 g tinned peaches
(drained weight), sliced

1 quantity Vanilla Frosting (page 11)

soft light brown sugar, to decorate
(optional)

*two 12-hole cupcake trays,
lined with 16 paper cases
(see note on page 4)*

Makes 16

Preheat the oven to 175°C (160°C fan)/Gas 4.

Put the flour, sugar, baking powder, salt and butter in a freestanding electric mixer with a paddle attachment (or use a handheld electric whisk) and beat on slow speed until you get a sandy consistency and everything is combined. Gradually pour in half the milk and beat until the milk is just incorporated.

Whisk the eggs, vanilla extract and remaining milk together in a separate bowl for a few seconds, then pour into the flour mixture and continue beating until just incorporated (scrape any unmixed ingredients from the side of the bowl with a rubber spatula). Continue mixing for a couple more minutes until the mixture is smooth. Do not overmix.

Divide the sliced peaches between the paper cases so that the base of each case is covered. Spoon the cupcake mixture on top until two-thirds full and bake in the preheated oven for 20–25 minutes, or until light golden and the sponge bounces back when touched. A skewer inserted in the centre should come out clean. Leave the cupcakes to cool for about 15 minutes in the trays before turning out onto a wire cooling rack to cool completely.

When the cupcakes are cold, spoon the Vanilla Frosting onto each cupcake, gently smoothing over with a palette knife and making a swirl of frosting on each one. Finish with a light sprinkling of soft light brown sugar, if using.

pumpkin cupcakes

These cupcakes are popular at Halloween and Thanksgiving. The light sprinkling of ground cinnamon over the Cream Cheese Frosting gives them a pretty finish.

240 g plain flour

280 g caster sugar

2 tablespoons baking powder

3 teaspoons ground cinnamon, plus extra to decorate

¼ teaspoon salt

80 g unsalted butter, at room temperature

240 ml whole milk

2 eggs

200 g tinned pumpkin purée

1 quantity Cream Cheese Frosting (page 11)

two 12-hole cupcake trays, lined with 16 paper cases (see note on page 4)

Makes 16

Preheat the oven to 175°C (160°C fan)/Gas 4.

Put the flour, sugar, baking powder, cinnamon, salt and butter in a freestanding electric mixer with a paddle attachment (or use a handheld electric whisk) and beat on slow speed until you get a sandy consistency and everything is combined. Gradually pour in the milk and beat until well mixed.

Add the eggs to the mix and beat well (scrape any unmixed ingredients from the side of the bowl with a rubber spatula). Stir in the pumpkin purée by hand until evenly dispersed.

Spoon the mixture into the paper cases until one-third full and bake in the preheated oven for about 18–20 minutes, or until light golden and the sponge bounces back when touched. Leave the cupcakes to cool for about 15 minutes in the trays before turning out onto a wire cooling rack to cool completely.

When the cupcakes are cold, spoon the Cream Cheese Frosting onto each cupcake, gently smoothing over with a palette knife and making a swirl of frosting on each one. Finish with a light sprinkling of cinnamon.

toffee apple and gunpowder tea cupcakes

We created these for Guy Fawkes's Day, with toffee apple giving an autumnal feel to the cupcakes and gunpowder tea for that added... bang!

240 ml whole milk

3 gunpowder green tea bags (or regular green tea bags)

240 g plain flour

280 g caster sugar

1 tablespoon baking powder

¼ teaspoon salt

80 g unsalted butter, at room temperature

2 large eggs

toffee apple filling

2 sweet eating apples, such as Pink Lady, peeled, cored and roughly chopped

20 g unsalted butter

15 g soft light brown sugar

¼ teaspoon ground cinnamon, plus extra to decorate (optional)

1 tablespoon water

caramel

40 g soft dark brown sugar

40 g unsalted butter

40 ml double cream

caramel frosting

1 quantity caramel (see above)

280 g cream cheese, cold

500 g icing sugar, sifted

two 12-hole deep muffin trays, lined with 16 paper cases (see note on page 4)

Makes 16

Put the milk and tea bags in a jug, cover and refrigerate for four to five hours, or overnight if possible.

Preheat the oven to 175°C (160°C fan)/Gas 4.

Put the flour, sugar, baking powder, salt and butter in a freestanding electric mixer with a paddle attachment (or use a handheld electric whisk) and beat on slow speed until you get a sandy consistency and everything is well combined.

Remove the tea bags from the infused milk, wring out and discard. Slowly pour half the milk into the flour mixture and beat on a medium-slow speed until it is just incorporated. Whisk the eggs into the remaining milk, then pour into the flour mixture and continue beating until just incorporated (scrape any unmixed ingredients from the side of the bowl with a rubber spatula). The mixture will be quite runny.

Spoon the mixture into the paper cases until about one-third full and bake in the preheated oven for 18–20 minutes until the sponge bounces back when touched. A skewer inserted into the centre should come out clean. Leave the cupcakes to cool in the trays for about 15 minutes before turning out onto a wire cooling rack to cool completely.

For the toffee apple filling: Put all the ingredients in a saucepan, cover and cook over a low heat until the apples are very soft, about 12–15 minutes. Mash the mixture, then lay out on a baking tray, cover with clingfilm and refrigerate until cool.

For the caramel: Put the sugar and butter in a saucepan over a low heat and heat until melted, stirring continuously. Continue to cook over a low heat, stirring regularly, until the mixture thickens, about three to four minutes. Remove from the heat and pour in the cream, whisking continuously until well combined and smooth. Leave to cool to room temperature.

For the caramel frosting: Beat together the caramel, cream cheese and icing sugar in a freestanding electric mixer with a paddle attachment (or use a handheld electric whisk) on slow speed until well mixed. Turn the mixer up to medium speed and beat until the frosting is light and fluffy, about two minutes. Be careful not to overmix, or the cheese will split and the frosting will become runny.

When the cupcakes are cold, use a sharp knife to hollow out a small section in the centre of each cake, approximately 2 cm in diameter and 3 cm deep. Keep the sponge pieces. Spoon the apple filling into a piping bag and pipe into the hollows, then top with the sponge pieces. If you have any filling left, spread it thinly over the top of each cake, making sure not to go over the edges.

Spoon the frosting onto each cupcake, gently smoothing over with a palette knife and making a swirl of frosting on each one. Finish with a light sprinkling of cinnamon, if using.

marshmallow cupcakes

Very sweet and gooey, you can use either Chocolate or Vanilla frosting to top these cupcakes, with bits of marshmallow to give texture. Decorate with your choice of sprinkles and edible glitter!

240 g plain flour

280 g caster sugar

3 teaspoons baking powder

¼ teaspoon salt

90 g unsalted butter, at room temperature

240 ml whole milk

2 eggs

½ teaspoon vanilla extract

16 medium pink marshmallows

150 g mini marshmallows, for the frosting

1 quantity Vanilla Frosting (page 11)

edible glitter, to decorate

two 12-hole cupcake trays, lined with 16 paper cases (see note on page 4)

Makes 16

Preheat the oven to 175°C (160°C fan)/Gas 4.

Put the flour, sugar, baking powder, salt and butter in a freestanding electric mixer with a paddle attachment (or use a handheld electric whisk) and beat on slow speed until you get a sandy consistency and everything is combined. Gradually pour in half the milk and beat until the milk is just incorporated.

Whisk the eggs, vanilla extract and remaining milk together in a separate bowl for a few seconds, then pour into the flour mixture and continue beating until just incorporated (scrape any unmixed ingredients from the side of the bowl with a rubber spatula). Continue mixing for a couple more minutes until the mixture is smooth. Do not overmix.

Spoon the mixture into the paper cases until one-third full and bake in the preheated oven for 20–25 minutes, or until light golden and the sponge bounces back when touched. A skewer inserted in the centre should come out clean. Leave the cupcakes to cool for about 15 minutes in the trays before turning out onto a wire cooling rack to cool completely.

Put the medium marshmallows in a heatproof bowl over a pan of simmering water. Remove from the heat as the marshmallows begin to melt and stir off the heat until they have all melted. When the cupcakes are cold, use a sharp knife to hollow out a small section in the centre of each cake, approximately 2 cm in diameter and 3 cm deep. Keep the sponge pieces. Fill with a dollop of melted marshmallow using two teaspoons dipped in hot water to scoop the melted marshmallows from the bowl. Top with the sponge pieces and leave to cool.

Stir the mini marshmallows into the Vanilla Frosting by hand until evenly dispersed.

Spoon the frosting onto each cupcake, gently smoothing over with a palette knife and making a swirl of frosting on each one. Decorate with edible glitter.

ginger cupcakes

A spicy cupcake, moistened with ginger syrup, perfect in winter. We've decorated ours with small pieces of chopped stem ginger and added lemon zest for that extra zing.

240 g plain flour

280 g caster sugar

3 teaspoons baking powder

1 teaspoon ground cinnamon

½ teaspoon ground allspice

¼ teaspoon salt

80 g unsalted butter,
at room temperature

240 ml whole milk

2 eggs

½ teaspoon vanilla extract

400 g stem ginger in syrup,
finely chopped (and syrup reserved),
plus extra to decorate

50 ml water

ginger frosting

75 ml whole milk

75 g fresh ginger, peeled and
chopped into 4 chunks

600 g icing sugar, sifted

190 g unsalted butter,
at room temperature

finely grated zest of 1 lemon,
plus extra to decorate

*two 12-hole cupcake trays,
lined with 16 paper cases
(see note on page 4)*

Makes 16

For the ginger frosting, put the milk and ginger pieces in a jug, cover and refrigerate for a few hours, or overnight if possible.

Preheat the oven to 175°C (160°C fan)/Gas 4.

Put the flour, sugar, baking powder, cinnamon, allspice, salt and butter in a freestanding electric mixer with a paddle attachment (or use a handheld electric whisk) and beat on slow speed until you get a sandy consistency and everything is combined. Slowly pour in half the milk and beat until just incorporated. Whisk the eggs, vanilla extract and remaining milk together in a separate bowl for a few seconds, then pour into the flour mixture and keep beating until just incorporated (scrape any unmixed ingredients from the side of the bowl with a rubber spatula). Continue mixing for a couple more minutes until the mixture is smooth. Stir in the chopped ginger by hand until evenly dispersed.

Spoon the mixture into the paper cases until half full and bake for 20–25 minutes, or until golden brown and the sponge bounces back when touched. Meanwhile, pour the water and 50 ml of the reserved ginger syrup into a small saucepan and bring to the boil. Boil until reduced by one-third. When the cupcakes come out of the oven, pour a small amount of syrup over each one. Leave the cupcakes to cool for about 15 minutes in the trays before turning out onto a wire cooling rack to cool completely.

For the ginger frosting: Beat together the icing sugar, butter and lemon zest in a freestanding electric mixer with a paddle attachment (or use a handheld electric whisk) on medium-slow speed until the mixture comes together and is well mixed. Turn the mixer down to slow speed. Strain the ginger-infused milk and slowly pour into the butter mixture. Once all the milk has been incorporated, turn the mixer up to high speed. Continue beating until the frosting is light and fluffy, at least five minutes.

Spoon the frosting on top, gently smoothing over with a palette knife and making a swirl of frosting on each one. Finish with chopped stem ginger and lemon zest.

cakes

hummingbird cake

Despite the name, we didn't invent this cake! It's a popular vintage recipe from the American South and is slightly similar to our carrot cake – moist and packed with flavour – but contains bananas and pineapple instead of carrots. The traditional recipe calls for pecan nuts, the quintessentially American nut, but walnuts could also be used.

300 g caster sugar

3 eggs

300 ml sunflower oil

270 g peeled bananas, mashed

1 teaspoon ground cinnamon, plus extra to decorate

300 g plain flour

1 teaspoon bicarbonate of soda

½ teaspoon salt

¼ teaspoon vanilla extract

100 g tinned pineapple (drained weight), chopped into small pieces

100 g shelled pecan nuts (or walnuts), chopped, plus 50 g extra, chopped and whole, to decorate

1 quantity Cream Cheese Frosting (page 11)

three 20-cm sandwich cake tins, base-lined with greaseproof paper

Makes one 20-cm cake, to slice as desired

Preheat the oven to 175°C (160°C fan)/Gas 4.

Put the sugar, eggs, oil, bananas and cinnamon in a freestanding electric mixer with a paddle attachment (or use a handheld electric whisk) and beat until all the ingredients are well incorporated (don't worry if the mixture looks slightly split). Slowly add the flour, bicarbonate of soda, salt and vanilla extract and continue to beat until everything is well mixed.

Stir in the chopped pineapple and pecan nuts by hand until evenly dispersed.

Pour the mixture into the prepared cake tins and smooth over with a palette knife. Bake in the preheated oven for 20–25 minutes, or until golden brown and the sponge bounces back when touched. Leave the cakes to cool for about ten minutes in the tins before turning out onto a wire cooling rack to cool completely.

When the cakes are cold, put one on a cake stand and spread about one-quarter of the Cream Cheese Frosting over it with a palette knife. Place a second cake on top and spread another quarter of the frosting over it. Top with the last cake and spread the remaining frosting over the top and sides. Finish with the extra pecan nuts and a light sprinkling of cinnamon.

mile high chocolate salted caramel cake

A rich chocolate sponge with a salted caramel filling make this a showstopper bake. Decorate with caramel curls which you can buy online, or grate some dark chocolate over the top.

400 g plain flour

645 g caster sugar

180 g cocoa powder

1 tablespoon bicarbonate of soda

1½ teaspoons baking powder

1½ teaspoons salt

4 large eggs

2 teaspoons vanilla extract

120 ml vegetable oil

410 ml buttermilk

250 ml water

caramel curls, to decorate (optional)

salted caramel filling

290 g caster sugar

35 g golden syrup

20 ml water

160 ml double cream

1 teaspoon salt

80 g unsalted butter, at
room temperature

chocolate frosting

400 g icing sugar, sifted

100 g cocoa powder

160 g unsalted butter, at room
temperature

75 ml whole milk

*three 20-cm sandwich cake tins, greased
and base-lined with greaseproof paper*

sugar thermometer

**Makes one 20-cm cake, to slice
as desired**

For the salted caramel filling: Put the sugar, golden syrup and water in a large saucepan over medium heat and heat until the sugar has dissolved and the liquid is a rich auburn colour. Don't stir, otherwise crystals will form. Remove from the heat and slowly add the cream, whisking continuously. The mixture will splatter so be very careful not to get splashed with hot syrup. Whisk until the mixture is smooth.

Put the pan over a medium heat and bring the caramel to 115°C (240°F) on a sugar thermometer: the 'soft ball' stage (page 98). Pour into a heatproof bowl and stir in the sea salt. Leave to cool for 10–15 minutes, then stir the butter into the caramel. Lay clingfilm directly on top (to stop a skin forming) and set aside.

Preheat the oven to 175°C (fan 160C)/Gas 4.

Put the flour, sugar, cocoa powder, bicarbonate of soda, baking powder and salt in a freestanding electric mixer with a paddle attachment (or use a handheld electric whisk) and beat on slow speed. Put the eggs, vanilla extract, oil, buttermilk and water into a jug and mix until just combined. Slowly pour into the flour mixture, mixing well and scraping any unmixed ingredients from the side of the bowl with a rubber spatula. Turn the mixer up to medium speed and beat for a couple more minutes until smooth, but don't overbeat.

Pour the mixture into the prepared cake tins and smooth over with a palette knife. Bake in the preheated oven for 30–35 minutes, or until the sponge bounces back when touched. A skewer inserted in the centre should come out clean. Leave the cakes to cool for 15 minutes in the tins before turning out onto wire cooling racks to cool completely.

When the cakes are cold, using a serrated knife, slice each in half horizontally. Gently cut around the edge of the cake first and then through the centre.

For the frosting: Put the icing sugar, cocoa powder and butter in a freestanding electric mixer with a paddle attachment (or use a handheld electric whisk) and beat on slow speed until you get a slightly sandy consistency and everything is combined.

Slowly pour in the milk, then when it is all incorporated, turn the mixer up to high speed. Continue beating until the frosting is light and fluffy, at least five minutes.

Put a sponge layer onto a cake stand and spread about one-fifth (about 3 tablespoons) of the caramel filling over it with a palette knife. Place the other half of the same cake on top and spread another fifth of the filling over it. Repeat with another three sponge layers and the remaining filling. Top with the last layer (but don't put any caramel on this layer) and spread the frosting over the top and sides. Decorate with caramel curls, if using.

carrot cake

Another bestseller at The Hummingbird Bakery, this carrot cake is moist and full of flavour. You can vary how finely you chop the nuts for the sponge, and pecan nuts or walnuts can be substituted freely. For an extra special touch, decorate the top with mini carrots – these can either be formed by hand using sugar paste, or piped on using orange buttercream icing.

300 g soft light brown sugar

3 eggs

300 ml sunflower oil

300 g plain flour

1 teaspoon bicarbonate of soda

1 teaspoon baking powder

1 teaspoon ground cinnamon, plus extra to decorate

½ teaspoon ground ginger

½ teaspoon salt

¼ teaspoon vanilla extract

300 g carrots, grated

100 g shelled walnuts, chopped, plus 75 g extra, chopped and whole, to decorate

1 quantity Cream Cheese Frosting (page 11)

three 20-cm sandwich cake tins, greased and base-lined with greaseproof paper

Makes one 20-cm cake, to slice as desired

Preheat the oven to 175°C (160°C fan)/Gas 4.

Put the sugar, eggs and oil in a freestanding electric mixer with a paddle attachment (or use a handheld electric whisk) and beat until all the ingredients are well incorporated (don't worry if the mixture looks slightly split). Slowly add the flour, bicarbonate of soda, baking powder, cinnamon, ginger, salt and vanilla extract and continue to beat until well mixed.

Stir in the grated carrots and walnuts by hand until they are all evenly dispersed.

Pour the mixture into the prepared cake tins and smooth over with a palette knife. Bake in the preheated oven for 20–25 minutes, or until golden brown and the sponge bounces back when touched. Leave the cakes to cool for about ten minutes in the tins before turning out onto a wire cooling rack to cool completely.

When the cakes are cold, put one on a cake stand and spread about one-quarter of the Cream Cheese Frosting over it with a palette knife. Place a second cake on top and spread another quarter of the frosting over it. Top with the last cake and spread the remaining frosting over the top and sides. Finish with the extra walnuts and a light sprinkling of cinnamon.

grasshopper cake

This cake has 'naked' edges, to show off the chocolate layers and custard filling.

235 ml whole milk

2 peppermint tea bags

115 g unsalted butter, at room temperature

35 g vegetable shortening, such as Trex or Cookeen

390 g caster sugar

3 large eggs

2 teaspoons vanilla extract

265 g plain flour

70 g cocoa powder

1 teaspoon baking powder

1 teaspoon bicarbonate of soda

½ teaspoon salt

5 chocolate cookies, to decorate

chocolate and peppermint custard

500 ml whole milk

160 g caster sugar

4½ tablespoons cornflour

1 teaspoon peppermint extract

2 large eggs, plus 1 large egg yolk

125 g white chocolate, finely chopped

a couple of drops of green food colouring (optional)

50 g dark chocolate chips

whipped cream topping

300 ml whipping cream, cold

1 tablespoon icing sugar

½ teaspoon peppermint extract

two 20-cm sandwich cake tins, greased and base-lined with greaseproof paper

Makes one 20-cm cake, to slice as desired

Put the 235 ml milk in a saucepan over a medium-high heat and heat until small bubbles form at the edges, but don't let the milk boil. Add the tea bags and leave to cool and steep for at least two hours, longer if possible.

For the chocolate and peppermint custard: Put the milk in a medium saucepan over a medium heat and bring to a simmer. Put the sugar, cornflour, peppermint extract, eggs and egg yolk in a medium heatproof bowl and whisk until smooth and well mixed. Slowly whisk half the hot milk into the egg mixture to combine. Pour the remaining milk into the egg mixture, then pour everything back into the saucepan, turn the heat down to medium-low and bring to the boil, whisking continuously with a balloon whisk. Reduce the heat to a simmer and cook for two to three minutes, whisking continuously until the mixture thickens and coats the back of a spoon. Pour the custard into a bowl. Don't worry if it's a bit lumpy, you can pass it through a fine sieve to get out any lumps if necessary.

Stir in the white chocolate and the food colouring, if using, until the chocolate melts. Lay clingfilm directly on top (to stop a skin forming) and refrigerate for at least two and a half hours until cold. When cold, fold in the chocolate chips and set aside.

Preheat the oven to 175°C (160°C fan)/Gas 4.

Put the butter and shortening in a freestanding electric mixer with a paddle attachment (or use a handheld electric whisk) and beat on medium speed for a few minutes to loosen up. Turn the mixer up to high speed, add the sugar and beat until light and fluffy, four to five minutes. Turn the mixer down to slower speed and add the eggs one at a time, mixing well and scraping any unmixed ingredients from the side of the bowl with a rubber spatula after each addition. Beat in the vanilla extract until well mixed.

Remove the tea bags from the infused milk, wring out and discard. Sift the flour, cocoa powder, baking powder, bicarbonate of soda and salt into a separate bowl. Add one-third of the flour mixture to the butter mixture, followed by half the infused milk. Mix well. Repeat this process, then finish with the remaining flour mixture.

Pour the mixture into the prepared cake tins and smooth over with a palette knife. Bake in the preheated oven for about 30–35 minutes, or until the sponges bounce back when touched. Leave the cakes to cool for about ten minutes in the tins before turning out onto wire cooling racks to cool completely.

When the cakes are cold, using a serrated knife, slice them in half horizontally.

For the whipped cream topping: Put the cream, icing sugar and peppermint extract in a freestanding electric mixer with a whisk attachment (or use a handheld electric whisk) and beat until stiff peaks form.

 Put a sponge layer onto a cake stand and spread about one-third of the custard over it with a palette knife, stopping about 1.5 cm from the edge. Place a second layer on top and spread another third of the custard over it. Repeat with another sponge layer and the remaining custard. Top with the last layer and spread the cream topping over the top. Decorate with the crushed cookies.

See photograph on pages 64–65.

coconut meringue cake

Containing fresh coconut, this is the ultimate coconut cake. No yolks are used in the sponge, making it airy and lighter (freeze the yolks with a pinch of salt to make ice cream or custard later). The boiled, soft meringue icing is as light as the sponge, and sprinkling grated coconut all over makes it look extra special.

1 fresh coconut (yielding about 200 g when grated)

water, as needed

430 g caster sugar

120 g unsalted butter, at room temperature

500 g plain flour

1 tablespoon baking powder

250 ml whole milk

1 teaspoon vanilla extract

3 egg whites

meringue frosting

200 g egg whites (from 6–7 eggs)

320 g caster sugar

75 ml water

¼ teaspoon vanilla extract

three 20-cm sandwich cake tins, greased and base-lined with greaseproof paper

Makes one 20-cm cake, to slice as desired

Preheat the oven to 175°C (160°C fan)/Gas 4.

Pierce the eyes of the coconut and strain the milk into a jug. Add water to make 250 ml and pour into a saucepan. Add 60 g sugar and bring to the boil, then simmer for two to three minutes, stirring frequently. When it has reduced to about 175 ml syrup, set aside to cool. Meanwhile, heat the drained coconut in the oven for about 15 minutes. Crack open the coconut and scoop out the fruit. Trim off the skin with a sharp knife. Grate the coconut and set aside.

Put the butter and remaining sugar in a freestanding electric mixer with a paddle attachment (or use a handheld electric whisk) and cream until light and fluffy. In a separate bowl, mix the flour and baking powder. In another bowl, mix the milk and vanilla extract. Beat the flour mixture into the creamed butter alternately with the milk mixture (scrape any unmixed ingredients from the sides with a rubber spatula). Beat until well mixed. In yet another bowl, whisk the egg whites with a handheld electric whisk until stiff peaks form. Using a metal spoon, stir in one-quarter of the egg whites to loosen the cake mixture, then fold in the remainder until well mixed but do not overmix. Pour into the prepared cake tins and smooth over with a palette knife. Bake in the oven for 25–30 minutes. Leave to cool for about ten minutes in the tins before turning out onto a wire cooling rack to cool.

For the meringue frosting: Put the egg whites, sugar and water in a heatproof bowl over a saucepan of simmering water. Beat slowly with an electric handheld whisk until stiff peaks form, about 10–12 minutes. Remove from the heat and beat in the vanilla extract. The frosting should be thick and glossy.

When the cakes are cold, put one on a serving plate and drizzle with coconut syrup. Spread one-fifth of the frosting over it with a palette knife and top with grated coconut. Repeat for the next cake, then top with the third and spread the remaining frosting over the top and sides. Cover with grated coconut.

chocolate cola cake

So many vintage American recipes call for soft drinks as an ingredient, and this makes sense, giving moisture, tang and sweetness to the resulting bake. Make sure you don't use the sugar-free version of your favourite cola brand, as this will mar the flavour of the cake.

350 ml cola (not diet)

175 g unsalted butter, at room temperature

180 ml vegetable oil

35 g cocoa powder

645 g caster sugar

400 g plain flour

125 g marshmallow fluff (or mini, white marshmallows)

1½ teaspoons bicarbonate of soda

180 ml buttermilk

3 eggs

1½ teaspoons vanilla extract

50 g pecan halves, to decorate

cola frosting

230 g unsalted butter, at room temperature

50 g cocoa powder

180 ml cola (not diet)

2 teaspoons vanilla extract

900 g icing sugar, sifted

three 20-cm sandwich cake tins, greased and base-lined with greaseproof paper

Makes one 20-cm cake, to slice as desired

For the cola frosting: Put the butter, cocoa powder, cola and vanilla extract in a saucepan and bring to the boil over a low heat until melted and smooth. Remove from the heat.

Put the icing sugar into a freestanding electric mixer with a paddle attachment (or use a handheld electric whisk) and slowly pour in the hot cola mixture in a steady stream on slow speed until well combined and smooth. The frosting will be runny and warm. Refrigerate for about three to four hours until cool (the frosting will harden and the colour might darken, but this is normal).

Preheat the oven to 175°C (160°C fan)/Gas 4.

Put the cola, butter, oil and cocoa powder into a saucepan and bring to the boil over low heat until melted and smooth.

Put the sugar, flour and marshmallow fluff (or mini marshmallows) into a freestanding electric mixer with a paddle attachment (or use a handheld electric whisk). Slowly pour in the hot cola mixture on slow speed and mix until well incorporated. Put the bicarbonate of soda and buttermilk into a jug and mix to combine, then slowly pour into the marshmallow mixture.

Add the eggs one at a time, mixing well and scraping any unmixed ingredients from the side of the bowl with a rubber spatula after each addition. Add the vanilla extract, turn the mixer up to medium speed and beat for another minute until well combined and smooth.

Pour the mixture into the prepared cake tins and smooth over with a palette knife. Bake in the preheated oven for 35–40 minutes. A skewer inserted in the centre should come out clean (the tops will appear gooey because of the marshmallow, but the cakes will firm as they cool). Leave the cakes to cool for about five minutes in the tins before turning out onto wire cooling racks to cool completely.

When the cakes are cold, take the frosting out of the fridge, put in a freestanding electric mixer with a paddle attachment (or use a handheld electric whisk) and beat for about three to four minutes until thickened, pale and fluffy (it will be a little thicker than a normal buttercream).

Put one cake on a cake stand and spread one-quarter of the frosting over with a palette knife. Place a second cake on top and spread another quarter of the frosting over it. Top with the last cake and spread the remaining frosting over the top and sides. Finish with pecan nuts, if using.

brooklyn blackout cake

This is a must for chocolate lovers, made famous by the now-defunct Ebinger's Bakery in Brooklyn. The filling and icing is made from an eggless chocolate custard which you must spread on a thin tray, covered with clingfilm to cool down quickly. The cake looks amazing when covered with crumbled chocolate sponge, with the almost black custard peeking through. Refrigerate the cake to set slightly before serving.

100 g unsalted butter, at room temperature

260 g caster sugar

2 eggs

¼ teaspoon vanilla extract

45 g cocoa powder

¾ teaspoon baking powder

¾ teaspoon bicarbonate of soda

a pinch of salt

170 g plain flour

160 ml whole milk

chocolate custard

350 g caster sugar

½ tablespoon golden syrup

85 g cocoa powder

700 ml water, plus 75–90 ml for mixing with the cornflour

85 g cornflour

60 g unsalted butter, cubed

¼ teaspoon vanilla extract

three 20-cm sandwich cake tins, greased and base-lined with greaseproof paper

Makes one 20-cm cake, to slice as desired

Preheat the oven to 175°C (160°C fan)/Gas 4.

Put the butter and sugar in a freestanding electric mixer with a paddle attachment (or use a handheld electric whisk) and cream until light and fluffy. Add the eggs one at a time, mixing well and scraping any unmixed ingredients from the side of the bowl with a rubber spatula after each addition. Turn the mixer down to slow speed and beat in the vanilla extract, cocoa powder, baking powder, bicarbonate of soda and salt until well mixed. Add half the flour, then all the milk, and finish with the remaining flour. Mix well until well combined. Pour the mixture into the prepared cake tins and smooth over with a palette knife. Bake in the preheated oven for 20–25 minutes. Leave the cakes to cool for about ten minutes in the tins before turning out onto a wire cooling rack to cool completely.

For the chocolate custard: Put the sugar, golden syrup, cocoa powder and 700 ml water into a large saucepan and bring to the boil over a medium heat, whisking occasionally. Mix the cornflour with 75–90 ml water, whisking briskly as you add the water. The mixture should be the consistency of thick glue. Whisk gradually into the cocoa mixture in the pan over a medium (not high) heat. Bring back to the boil, whisking constantly. Cook, whisking constantly, for three to four minutes, until the mixture is glossy and coats the back of a spoon. Remove from the heat and stir in the butter until melted, then the vanilla extract. Pour into a bowl, cover with clingfilm and chill until very firm.

Slice a thin layer off one cake and put in a food processor. Process into fine crumbs. Put one cake on a cake stand and spread one-quarter of the custard over it. Place a second cake on top and spread another quarter of the custard over it. Top with the last cake and spread the remaining custard over the top and sides. Cover with the crumbs and chill for two hours.

lemon and poppy seed cake

A moist, tangy cake that is perfect with your afternoon cup of tea. If you don't have a Bundt® tin, then only fill whatever ring mould tin you have to a maximum of two-thirds full, otherwise the batter may erupt over the tin! If you have leftover batter, put it into muffin cases and make cupcakes.

85 g unsalted butter,
at room temperature

245 g caster sugar

finely grated zest of 1½ lemons

15 g poppy seeds,
plus extra to decorate

165 ml whole milk

235 g plain flour

2 teaspoons baking powder

½ teaspoon salt

3 egg whites

lemon syrup

freshly squeezed juice and finely
grated zest of 1 lemon

50 g caster sugar

100 ml water

lemon glaze

freshly squeezed juice of 1 lemon

250 g icing sugar, sifted

*a 25-cm Bundt® tin, greased and
dusted with flour*

**Makes one 25-cm cake,
to slice as desired**

Preheat the oven to 175°C (160°C fan)/Gas 4.

Put the butter, sugar, lemon zest and poppy seeds in a freestanding electric mixer with a paddle attachment (or use a handheld electric whisk) and beat until all the ingredients are well incorporated (don't worry if the mixture looks slightly split). Slowly add the milk and continue to beat until incorporated (don't worry if the mixture looks slightly split).

In a separate bowl, combine the flour, baking powder and salt. Add the flour mixture to the butter mixture in three stages, scraping any unmixed ingredients from the side of the bowl with a rubber spatula after each addition. Beat thoroughly until all the ingredients are well mixed and the mixture is light and fluffy.

In a separate bowl, whisk the egg whites with a handheld electric whisk until stiff peaks form. Using a metal spoon, gradually fold the whisked egg whites into the cake mixture until well mixed but do not overmix. Pour into the prepared ring mould and smooth over with a palette knife. Bake in the preheated oven for about 30 minutes, or until the sponge bounces back when touched and a skewer inserted comes out clean.

For the lemon syrup: While the cake is baking, put the lemon juice and zest, sugar and water in a small saucepan and bring to the boil over a low heat. Raise the heat and boil until it has reduced by half, or until it has a thin syrup consistency, about six to seven minutes. When the hot cake comes out of the oven, pour the syrup all over the top. Leave to cool slightly in the mould before turning out onto a wire cooling rack to cool completely.

For the lemon glaze: Mix the lemon juice and icing sugar in a bowl until smooth. It should be thick but pourable – add a little water or more sugar to thin or thicken as necessary.

When the cake is cold, put it on a cake stand, pour the glaze over it and decorate with poppy seeds.

blueberry cake

Blueberries work so well in cakes as they become soft and juicy and a wonderful deep purple. The blueberries will definitely sink towards the bottom of the cake as it bakes, this is normal. You can dust them in flour to slow the sinking down and definitely the faster you put the batter into the preheated oven the less they'll sink. This is moist enough to be served without the frosting if you prefer. Remember, only fill whatever ring mould you have to a maximum of two-thirds full to prevent a mess in your oven.

350 g unsalted butter,
at room temperature

350 g caster sugar

6 eggs

1 teaspoon vanilla extract

450 g plain flour

2 tablespoons plus 2 teaspoons baking powder

280 ml soured cream

250 g fresh blueberries,
plus extra to decorate

½ quantity Cream Cheese Frosting (page 11)

icing sugar, to decorate

a 25-cm Bundt® tin, greased and dusted with flour

**Makes one 25-cm cake,
to slice as desired**

Preheat the oven to 175°C (160°C fan)/Gas 4.

Put the butter and sugar in a freestanding electric mixer with a paddle attachment (or use a handheld electric whisk) and cream until light and fluffy. Add the eggs one at a time, mixing well and scraping any unmixed ingredients from the side of the bowl with a rubber spatula after each addition. Beat in the vanilla extract, flour and baking powder until well mixed. Add the soured cream and mix well until everything is combined and the mixture is light and fluffy.

Gently stir in the blueberries by hand until evenly dispersed.

Pour the mixture into the prepared ring mould and smooth over with a palette knife. Bake in the preheated oven for 55–60 minutes, or until golden brown and the sponge bounces back when touched. Leave the cake to cool for about ten minutes in the mould before turning out onto a wire cooling rack to cool completely.

When the cake is cold, put it on a serving plate, cover the top and sides with the Cream Cheese Frosting and decorate with more blueberries. Dust with a light sprinkling of icing sugar.

coffee cake

This is less sweet than some of the other cakes in this chapter, but you could top it with Chocolate Frosting to turn it into a mocha cake for a sweeter tooth. Remember, only fill whatever ring mould you have to a maximum of two-thirds full to prevent a mess in your oven.

2 tablespoons instant coffee granules

170 ml water

450 g unsalted butter,
at room temperature

450 g caster sugar

8 eggs

450 g plain flour

2 tablespoons baking powder

2 teaspoons cocoa powder,
plus extra to decorate

½ quantity Vanilla Frosting (page 11)

20 g dark chocolate, grated with a
cheese grater into shavings

coffee beans, to decorate (optional)

*a 25-cm Bundt® tin, greased and
dusted with flour*

**Makes one 25-cm cake,
to slice as desired**

To make a coffee essence, put the instant coffee granules and water in a small saucepan and bring to the boil over medium heat. Boil until reduced by half, then remove from the heat and leave to cool completely. Set aside a tablespoon of the essence to use in the frosting.

Preheat the oven to 175°C (160°C fan)/Gas 4.

Put the butter, sugar and cold coffee essence in a freestanding electric mixer with a paddle attachment (or use a handheld electric whisk) and beat until all the ingredients are well incorporated. Add the eggs one at a time, mixing well and scraping any unmixed ingredients from the side of the bowl with a rubber spatula after each addition. Beat in the flour, baking powder and cocoa powder and mix well until everything is combined and the mixture is light and fluffy.

Pour the mixture into the prepared ring mould and smooth over with a palette knife. Bake in the preheated oven for 40–50 minutes, or until the sponge feels firm to the touch. (Do not open the oven while the cake is baking, as it will sink.) Leave the cake to cool for about ten minutes in the mould before turning out onto a wire cooling rack to cool completely.

Stir the reserved tablespoon of coffee essence into the Vanilla Frosting until evenly mixed.

When the cake is cold, put it on a serving plate, cover the top with the frosting and dust with a light sprinkling of cocoa powder. Decorate with the chocolate shavings and coffee beans, if using.

spiced pound cake

This is more flavourful than a regular American pound cake, with lots of spices to liven it up. It's another not-too-sweet cake that's perfect with a cup of tea or coffee. Remember, only fill whatever ring mould you have to a maximum of two-thirds full to prevent a mess in your oven.

230 g unsalted butter,
at room temperature

650 g caster sugar

5 eggs

240 ml whole milk

1 teaspoon vanilla extract

¼ teaspoon lemon extract

¼ teaspoon ground cloves

¼ teaspoon ground cinnamon

¼ teaspoon ground ginger

¼ teaspoon ground nutmeg

400 g plain flour

½ teaspoon bicarbonate of soda

½ teaspoon salt

a 25-cm Bundt® tin, greased and dusted with flour

**Makes one 25-cm cake,
to slice as desired**

Preheat the oven to 175°C (160°C fan)/Gas 4.

Put the butter and sugar in a freestanding electric mixer with a paddle attachment (or use a handheld electric whisk) and cream until light and fluffy. Add the eggs one at a time, mixing well and scraping any unmixed ingredients from the side of the bowl with a rubber spatula after each addition. Beat in the milk, vanilla extract and lemon extract until well mixed.

Sift the cloves, cinnamon, ginger, nutmeg, flour, bicarbonate of soda and salt into a separate bowl, then add to the butter mixture and beat until all the ingredients are well combined.

Pour the mixture into the prepared ring mould and smooth over with a palette knife. Bake in the preheated oven for 60–70 minutes, or until golden brown and a skewer inserted in the cake comes out clean. Leave to cool for about ten minutes in the mould before turning out onto a wire cooling rack to cool completely.

buttermilk pound loaf

Here's a reliable, traditional pound cake recipe – moist with butter and not too sweet. You can add chocolate chips, nuts or berries to the batter as an alternative.

120 g unsalted butter,
at room temperature

330 g caster sugar

3 eggs

200 g plain flour

½ teaspoon bicarbonate of soda

½ teaspoon salt

120 ml buttermilk

¼ teaspoon vanilla extract

*a 900 g loaf tin, greased and
dusted with flour*

**Makes one loaf, to be sliced
as desired**

Preheat the oven to 170°C (155°C fan)/Gas 3½.

Put the butter and sugar in a freestanding electric mixer with a paddle attachment (or use a handheld electric whisk) and cream until light, soft and well combined. Add the eggs one at a time, mixing well and scraping any unmixed ingredients from the side of the bowl with a rubber spatula after each addition.

Sift the flour, bicarbonate of soda and salt into a separate bowl. Add one-third of the flour mixture to the butter mixture, followed by half the buttermilk. Mix well. Repeat this process, then finish with the remaining flour mixture. Stir in the vanilla extract. Mix well until all the ingredients are well combined.

Pour the mixture into the prepared loaf tin and smooth over with a palette knife. Bake in the preheated oven for 50 minutes–1 hour, or until golden brown and a skewer inserted in the sponge comes out clean. Leave the cake to cool for about ten minutes in the tin before turning out onto a wire cooling rack to cool completely.

banana loaf

This recipe has proved to be an all-time favourite with our home bakers! Try to use very ripe bananas for a sweeter, richer cake. You can also use light muscovado sugar, making the cake even more moist and rich.

270 g soft light brown sugar

2 eggs

200 g peeled bananas, mashed

280 g plain flour

1 teaspoon baking powder

1 teaspoon bicarbonate of soda

1 teaspoon ground cinnamon

1 teaspoon ground ginger

140 g unsalted butter, melted

a 900 g loaf tin, greased and dusted with flour

Makes one loaf, to be sliced as desired

Preheat the oven to 170°C (155°C fan)/Gas 3½.

Put the sugar and eggs in a freestanding electric mixer with a paddle attachment (or use a handheld electric whisk) and beat until well incorporated. Beat in the mashed bananas.

Add the flour, baking powder, bicarbonate of soda, cinnamon and ginger to the sugar mixture. Mix it thoroughly until all the dry ingredients have been incorporated into the egg mixture. Pour in the melted butter and beat until all the ingredients are well mixed.

Pour the mixture into the prepared loaf tin and smooth over with a palette knife. Bake in the preheated oven for about one hour, or until firm to the touch and a skewer inserted in the centre comes out clean. Leave the cake to cool for about ten minutes in the tin before turning out onto a wire cooling rack to cool completely.

nutty apple loaf

This cake is very popular in the winter months. We use chopped mixed nuts, but you could use your own combination of favourite nuts. The chunks of cooked apple in the cake give it a wonderful texture and flavour. Remember to let it cool completely before serving, and because it is so nutty, it's going to crumble slightly when slicing, so don't worry about that.

175 g unsalted butter, at room temperature

140 g soft light brown sugar

2 tablespoons strawberry jam

2 eggs

140 g plain flour

1 tablespoon baking powder

1 teaspoon ground cinnamon

100 g shelled unsalted mixed nuts, chopped

50 g dark chocolate, roughly chopped

2 eating apples, peeled, cored and roughly chopped

a 900 g loaf tin, greased and dusted with flour

Makes one loaf, to be sliced as desired

Put the butter, sugar and strawberry jam in a freestanding electric mixer with a paddle attachment (or use a handheld electric whisk) and cream until light and fluffy. Add the eggs one at a time, mixing well and scraping any unmixed ingredients from the side of the bowl with a rubber spatula after each addition.

Sift together the flour, baking powder and cinnamon in a separate bowl, then beat into the butter mixture. Stir the nuts, chocolate and apples into the mixture by hand until evenly dispersed. Cover and refrigerate for a few hours, or overnight if possible.

Preheat the oven to 170°C (155°C fan)/Gas 3½.

Pour the mixture into the prepared loaf tin and smooth over with a palette knife. Bake in the preheated oven for one hour to one hour ten minutes, or until brown and the sponge feels firm to the touch. A skewer inserted in the centre should come out clean, but for a little melted chocolate. Leave the cake to cool for about ten minutes in the tin before turning out onto a wire cooling rack to cool completely.

lemon loaf

When drizzled with the lemon syrup, this is incredibly moist, tangy and flies off our counter when served in the shop.

320 g caster sugar

3 eggs

finely grated zest of 2 lemons

350 g plain flour

1½ teaspoons baking powder

1 teaspoon salt

250 ml whole milk

½ teaspoon vanilla extract

200 g unsalted butter, melted

lemon syrup

freshly squeezed juice and finely grated zest of 1 lemon

50 g caster sugar

100 ml water

a 900 g loaf tin,
greased and dusted with flour

Makes one loaf, to be sliced as desired

Preheat the oven to 170°C (155°C fan)/Gas 3½.

Put the sugar, eggs and lemon zest in a freestanding electric mixer with a paddle attachment (or use a handheld electric whisk) and beat until well mixed.

Sift the flour, baking powder and salt into a separate bowl. Combine the milk and vanilla extract in another bowl. Add one-third of the flour mixture to the sugar mixture and beat well, then beat in one-third of the milk mixture. Repeat this process twice more until everything has been added. Turn the mixer up to high speed and beat until the mixture is light, smooth and everything is well incorporated.

Turn the mixer down to low speed, pour in the melted butter and beat until well incorporated.

Pour the mixture into the prepared loaf tin and bake in the preheated oven for about 1 hour 15 minutes, or until golden brown and the sponge bounces back when touched.

For the lemon syrup: While the cake is baking, put the lemon juice and zest, sugar and water in a small saucepan and bring to the boil over low heat. Raise the heat and boil until it has reduced by half, or until it has a thin syrup consistency.

When the hot cake comes out of the oven, put it on a wire cooling rack over a surface covered with foil, and pour the syrup all over the top. The excess syrup will run over the edges. Leave to cool for about ten minutes in the tin before turning out onto the wire cooling rack to cool completely.

new york cheesecake

A plain baked New York cheesecake is always extremely popular. It's important not to overbeat the ingredients, so stop mixing as soon as each ingredient you add is just incorporated. You may think the cake isn't fully baked when you take it out of the oven, but it will set into a perfect cheesecake overnight! You can also fold in chopped cookies, brownies or berries just before baking to make a flavoured cheesecake.

900 g cream cheese
190 g caster sugar
1 teaspoon vanilla extract
4 eggs

base

140 g plain flour
¼ teaspoon baking powder
50 g caster sugar
50 g unsalted butter
1 egg yolk

a 23-cm round springform cake tin, greased and base-lined with greaseproof paper

Makes one 23-cm cheesecake, to slice as desired

Preheat the oven to 150°C (135°C fan)/Gas 2.

For the base: Put the flour, baking powder, sugar and butter in a freestanding electric mixer with a paddle attachment (or use a handheld electric whisk) and beat until you get a sandy consistency.

Add the egg yolk and mix through – the mixture will still have a sandy consistency but it will be a little more moist. Press this mixture into the base of the prepared cake tin, using the ball of your hand or a tablespoon to flatten and compress it. It must be pressed down to form a dense base.

Bake in the preheated oven for 20–25 minutes, or until golden brown. It should have lost its sandy texture and come together to form a coherent base. Set aside to cool.

Put the cream cheese, sugar and vanilla extract in a freestanding electric mixer with a paddle attachment (or use a handheld electric whisk) and beat on slow speed until you get a very smooth, thick mixture. Add one egg at a time, while still mixing. Scrape any unmixed ingredients from the side of the bowl with a rubber spatula after adding each egg. The mixture should be very smooth and creamy. The mixer can be turned up to a higher speed at the end to make the mix a little lighter and fluffier, but be careful not to overmix otherwise the cheese will split.

Spoon the mixture onto the cold cheesecake base. Put the tin inside a larger tin or in a deep baking tray and fill with cold water until it reaches two-thirds of the way up the cake tin. Bake for 30–40 minutes, or until golden brown but still wobbly in the centre. Don't overcook. Leave the cheesecake to cool slightly in the tin, then cover and refrigerate overnight before serving.

chocolate cheesecake

There must be a chocolate version of everything so chocolate lovers don't have to miss out! Using the best quality dark chocolate in this cheesecake will make the finished result taste so much better. A mix of three kinds of chocolate chips (dark, milk and white) can be folded in before baking for an extra chocolate kick.

900 g cream cheese

190 g caster sugar

1 teaspoon vanilla extract

4 eggs

200 g dark chocolate, roughly chopped

base

200 g digestive biscuits

2 tablespoons cocoa powder

150 g unsalted butter, melted

a 23-cm round springform cake tin, greased and base-lined with greaseproof paper

Makes one 23-cm cheesecake, to slice as desired

Preheat the oven to 150°C (135°C fan)/Gas 2.

For the base: Roughly break up the digestive biscuits and put them in a food processor with the cocoa powder. Process until finely ground. Slowly pour the melted butter into the processor while the motor is running. Press this mixture into the base of the prepared cake tin, using the ball of your hand or the back of a tablespoon to flatten and compress it. Refrigerate while you make the topping.

Put the cream cheese, sugar and vanilla extract in a freestanding electric mixer with a paddle attachment (or use a handheld electric whisk) and beat on slow speed until you get a very smooth, thick mixture. Add one egg at a time, while still mixing. Scrape any unmixed ingredients from the side of the bowl with a rubber spatula after adding each egg. The mixture should be very smooth and creamy. The mixer can be turned up to a higher speed at the end to make the mix a little lighter and fluffier, but be careful not to overmix otherwise the cheese will split.

Put the chocolate in a heatproof bowl over a saucepan of simmering water (do not let the base of the bowl touch the water). Leave until melted and smooth, stirring occasionally. Spoon a little of the cream cheese mixture into the melted chocolate, stir to mix, then add a little more. This will even out the temperatures of the two mixtures. Eventually stir all the cream cheese mixture into the chocolate mixture and mix until well combined and smooth.

Spoon the mixture onto the cold cheesecake base. Put the tin inside a larger tin or in a deep baking tray and fill with cold water until it reaches two-thirds of the way up the cake tin. Bake for 40–50 minutes, checking regularly after 40 minutes to make sure it isn't burning. Don't overcook – it should be wobbly in the centre. Leave the cheesecake to cool slightly in the tin, then cover and refrigerate overnight before serving.

fridge-set banana cheesecake

This is another take on a cheesecake, but it is set and has a firmer texture than baked cheesecake. This recipe contains gelatine, so vegetarians will have to use a vegetarian alternative and follow the manufacturer's instructions.

6 gelatine leaves

200 g peeled bananas, mashed, plus 1 extra, sliced, to decorate

70 ml orange juice

300 g cream cheese

110 g caster sugar

3 egg yolks

250 ml double cream

base

200 g digestive biscuits

150 g unsalted butter, melted

a 23-cm round springform cake tin, greased and base-lined with greaseproof paper

Makes one 23-cm cheesecake, to slice as desired

For the base: Roughly break up the digestive biscuits and put them in a food processor. Process until finely ground. Slowly pour the melted butter into the processor while the motor is running. Press this mixture into the base of the prepared cake tin, using the ball of your hand or the back of a tablespoon to flatten and compress it. Refrigerate while you make the topping.

Put the gelatine leaves in a small jug of barely tepid water and soak according to the manufacturer's instructions.

Put the mashed bananas and orange juice in a saucepan and heat over a medium heat for about five to six minutes until the mixture is amalgamated and less lumpy. Set aside to cool slightly.

Put the cream cheese, sugar and egg yolks in a freestanding electric mixer with a paddle attachment (or use a handheld electric whisk) and beat on slow speed until you get a very smooth, thick mixture.

In a separate bowl, using a handheld electric whisk, whip the cream until thick but not stiff. Gently fold into the cream cheese mixture by hand. Set aside.

Take the soaked gelatine leaves out of the jug and put into the warm banana and orange juice mixture – make sure the banana mixture is just warm and not hot, as high heat can destroy the gelatine. Stir well until all the gelatine has completely melted and is evenly dispersed. Spoon a little of the cream cheese mixture into the banana mixture and stir to mix, then add a little more. This will even out the temperatures of the two mixtures and prevent the gelatine from setting in lumps. Eventually stir all the banana mixture into the cream cheese mixture and mix until well combined and smooth.

Spoon the mixture onto the cold cheesecake base and leave to cool completely. Cover and refrigerate for two hours, or overnight if possible. Decorate with slices of banana before serving.

pies

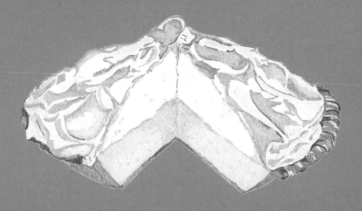

basic pie crust

This simple American flaky pie crust is used in most of the recipes in this chapter. You will either need to bake it blind and top with a pie filling which doesn't need any further baking, or, if the filling needs to be cooked, then only partially blind bake the crust. Remember: keep everything cold and don't handle the mixture too much.

180 g plain flour, plus extra to dust
120 g unsalted butter, cold
3 tablespoons water, plus extra if needed

a 23-cm pie dish, greased
baking beans

Makes enough for a 23-cm pie dish

Put the flour and butter in an electric mixer with a paddle attachment and beat on slow speed until you get a sandy consistency and everything is combined. Add 2 tablespoons water and beat until well mixed. Add a third tablespoon of water and beat until you have a smooth, even dough. If the dough is still a little dry, add another tablespoon of water, but be careful not to add too much water – it is safer to beat the dough at high speed to try to bring the ingredients together.

Wrap the dough in clingfilm and leave to rest for one hour.

Preheat the oven to 175°C (160°C fan)/Gas 4.

Lightly dust a clean work surface with flour and roll out the dough with a rolling pin to about 2 mm thickness. Line the prepared pie dish with the dough and trim the edges with a sharp knife. Lay a sheet of greaseproof paper over the pastry crust and pour in the baking beans.

To blind bake (for a pie that WILL NOT need baking again): Bake the pie crust in the preheated oven for about 15–20 minutes, or until the edges are light golden and partially cooked. Remove the greaseproof paper and baking beans and bake for a further 15–20 minutes. Take care not to overcook – the edges should be light golden.

To partially blind bake (for a pie that WILL need baking again): Bake the pie crust in the preheated oven for about ten minutes. Remove the greaseproof paper and baking beans and bake for a further ten minutes. The dough should still be pale and slightly raw in the centre.

lemon meringue pie

This old favourite never lasts long when we put it out on our shelves! The meringue topping should be generous and tall. There are two options for making the meringue in the recipe below: the Italian is our authentic version, but the nervous baker can use the simpler version. Use a warm knife when cutting the pie – it keeps the slices neat. The sliced cake look amazing with the bright yellow filling and white, fluffy topping.

8 egg yolks

2 x 397 g tins condensed milk

250 ml freshly squeezed juice and finely grated zest of 3 lemons

1 Basic Pie Crust, partially blind baked (opposite)

EITHER simple meringue topping

7 egg whites

265 g caster sugar

1 teaspoon vanilla extract

OR Italian meringue topping

400 g caster sugar

water, as needed

5 egg whites

¼ teaspoon vanilla extract

a 23-cm pie dish, greased

Makes one 23-cm pie, to slice as desired

Preheat the oven to 150°C (135°C fan)/Gas 2.

Put the egg yolks, condensed milk and lemon juice and zest in a glass bowl and mix gently with a balloon whisk until all the ingredients are very well incorporated. The mixture will thicken naturally.

Pour into the partially blind-baked pie crust and bake in the preheated oven for 20–30 minutes. The filling should be firm to the touch but still very slightly soft in the centre (not wobbly!). Leave to cool completely, then cover and refrigerate for at least one hour, or overnight if possible.

For the simple meringue topping: Preheat the oven to 150°C (135°C fan)/Gas 2.

Put the egg whites in a freestanding electric mixer with a whisk attachment and whisk until frothy. Gradually add 2 tablespoons of the sugar at a time, whisking well after each addition. Once you have whisked in all the sugar, add the vanilla extract and whisk again until stiff peaks form.

Spoon the meringue on top of the cold pie, making sure you completely cover the pie filling. Create peaks and swirls in the top of the meringue with the back of a tablespoon.

Bake in the preheated oven for about 20–25 minutes, or until the meringue is golden brown and crisp to the touch. (With this method, the egg whites are not cooked through, so please see the note on page 4 about uncooked or partially cooked eggs.) Leave to cool completely before serving.

For the Italian meringue topping: Preheat the oven to 150°C (135°C fan)/Gas 2.

Put the sugar in a small saucepan and just cover with water. Set over a medium heat and bring to the boil.

While the sugar is on the hob, put the egg whites in a freestanding electric mixer with a whisk attachment (or use a handheld electric whisk) on medium-slow speed. Whisk until the egg whites are light and foamy. When the sugar has been boiling for a short while, it should reach 'soft ball' stage (see below).

Turn the mixer up to medium-high speed and slowly pour the sugar syrup into the egg whites. Once all the syrup is incorporated, turn the mixer up to maximum speed and whisk for about 10–15 minutes, or until the meringue has tripled in size and is very white and fluffy. Turn the mixer back down to medium speed and continue to whisk for a couple more minutes until the meringue has cooled down slightly.

Spoon the meringue on top of the cold pie, making sure you completely cover the pie filling. Create peaks and swirls in the top of the meringue with the back of a tablespoon.

Bake in the preheated oven for about 20 minutes, or until the meringue is golden brown and crisp to the touch. Leave to cool completely before serving.

'Soft ball' stage: When the sugar has been boiling for a short while, the appearance of the bubbles starts to change from very watery to more syrupy. Using a sugar thermometer, the temperature should be about 115°C/240°F. Dip a spoon into the sugar, then drop it directly into a glass of cold water. The sugar will firm up on contact with the water. You should be able to form a soft ball out of the sugar, in which case it has reached soft ball stage. If it sets too hard to be able to form a ball, it has been boiled too long and has reached 'hard ball' stage. Be careful, as the sugar goes from soft ball stage to hard ball stage very quickly. Don't touch the hot syrup with your bare hands until you have dipped the spoon into the glass of cold water, otherwise you will burn your fingers!

pecan pie

Here's another American must. We've rejigged the recipe to use easier-to-find golden syrup and are happy to report that it now tastes exactly as if you used American dark corn syrup! This pie must cool down completely before you slice, to prevent a gooey mess in your pie dish.

1 quantity Basic Pie Crust dough, unbaked (page 96)

plain flour, to dust

100 g light brown sugar

100 g caster sugar

340 g golden syrup

¼ teaspoon salt

3 eggs

60 g unsalted butter

¼ teaspoon vanilla extract

100 g shelled pecan nuts, chopped, plus extra 100 g pecan halves to decorate

a 23-cm pie dish, greased

Makes one 23-cm pie, to slice as desired

Preheat the oven to 175°C (160°C fan)/Gas 4.

Lightly dust a clean work surface with flour and roll out the dough with a rolling pin. Line the prepared pie dish with the dough and trim the edges with a sharp knife.

Put the sugars, golden syrup and salt in a large saucepan over a medium heat. Bring to the boil, then remove from the heat and leave to cool down slightly.

In a separate bowl, whisk the eggs briefly with a balloon whisk until they are just mixed. Slowly pour the warm (not hot) syrup into the eggs, whisking briskly so that you don't allow the eggs time to scramble.

Add the butter and vanilla extract to the bowl and stir until the butter has melted and is evenly dispersed.

Put the chopped pecan nuts into the pie crust, then pour the filling on top. Arrange the pecan halves gently on top around the edge of the pie. Bake in the preheated oven for about 45–55 minutes, or until a dark, caramel colour with a slightly crusty surface.

key lime pie

We don't use any food colouring in our lime filling, just a bit of lime zest, so it's not green. Our Key Lime Pie is topped with a mound of freshly whipped cream, however you can use either of the meringues used for the Lemon Meringue Pie (see page 97).

8 egg yolks

2 x 397 g tins condensed milk

100 ml freshly squeezed juice and finely grated zest of 5 limes, plus extra finely grated zest to decorate

450 ml whipping cream

crust

300 g digestive biscuits

150 g unsalted butter, melted

a 23-cm pie dish, greased

Makes one 23-cm pie, to slice as desired

Preheat the oven to 175°C (160°C fan)/Gas 4.

For the crust: Roughly break up the digestive biscuits and put them in a food processor. Process until finely ground. Slowly pour the melted butter into the processor while the motor is running. Press this mixture into the base and neatly up the side of the prepared pie dish, using the ball of your hand or the back of a tablespoon to flatten and compress it.

Bake in the preheated oven for about 20 minutes, or until the digestives look baked and the base feels firm. Set aside to cool completely.

Turn the oven down to 150°C (fan135°C)/Gas 2.

Put the egg yolks, condensed milk and lime juice and zest in a glass bowl and mix gently with a balloon whisk until all the ingredients are very well incorporated. The mixture will thicken naturally.

Pour into the cold pie crust and bake in the preheated oven for 20–30 minutes. The filling should be firm to the touch but still very slightly soft in the centre (not wobbly!). Leave to cool completely, then cover and refrigerate for at least one hour, or overnight if possible.

When you are ready to serve the pie, whip the cream with a handheld electric whisk in a large bowl until soft peaks form, then spread over the pie and decorate with a little lime zest.

pumpkin pie

The classic Thanksgiving pie, Pumpkin Pie is incredibly easy to make. The finished pie looks rustic and simple, with a deep golden-orange filling. If you don't want to leave it plain, you can cover it in whipped cream, but plain is more traditional. You could bake fresh pumpkin if you can't find tinned, but the result is never as good.

1 Basic Pie Crust, partially blind baked (page 96)

1 egg

425 g tin pumpkin purée

300 ml evaporated milk

160 g caster sugar

¼ teaspoon ground cloves

½ teaspoon salt

1 teaspoon ground cinnamon, plus extra to decorate

½ teaspoon ground ginger

1 tablespoon plain flour, plus extra to dust

lightly whipped cream, to serve (optional)

a 23-cm pie dish, greased

Makes one 23-cm pie, to slice as desired

Preheat the oven to 175°C (160°C fan)/Gas 4.

Lightly dust a clean work surface with flour and roll out the dough with a rolling pin. Line the prepared pie dish with the pastry and trim the edges with a sharp knife.

Put the egg, pumpkin purée, evaporated milk, sugar, cloves, salt, cinnamon, ginger and flour in a large bowl and mix with a wooden spoon until everything is well combined and there are no lumps.

Pour into the pie crust and bake in the preheated oven for about 30–40 minutes, or until the filling is set firm and doesn't wobble when shaken.

Leave to cool completely, then serve with a dollop of lightly whipped cream, if using, and a light sprinkling of cinnamon.

mississippi mud pie

Our version of Mississippi Mud Pie has a rich, cooked chocolate pudding filling, topped with a mountain of whipped cream. You can top the pie with grated chocolate or dust with cocoa powder. This is another pie that is extremely popular and sells out fast. You must use dark (70% cocoa solids) chocolate otherwise the chocolate pudding filling won't set properly.

150 g dark chocolate, roughly chopped, plus extra, shaved with a vegetable peeler, to decorate

50 g unsalted butter

30 ml golden syrup

6 eggs

300 g soft light brown sugar

1 teaspoon vanilla extract

1 Basic Pie Crust, partially blind baked (page 96)

350 ml whipping cream

a 23-cm pie dish, greased

Makes one 23-cm pie, to slice as desired

Preheat the oven to 175°C (160°C fan)/Gas 4.

Put the chocolate, butter and golden syrup in a heatproof bowl over a saucepan of simmering water (do not let the base of the bowl touch the water). Leave until melted and smooth, then remove from the heat and leave to cool slightly.

While the chocolate mixture is melting, put the eggs, sugar and vanilla extract in a freestanding electric mixer with a paddle attachment (or use a handheld electric whisk) and beat until well combined.

Gradually beat the warm chocolate mixture into the egg mixture on slow speed. Make sure the chocolate isn't too hot, otherwise it will scramble the eggs. Beat thoroughly until smooth.

Pour into the partially blind-baked pie crust and bake in the preheated oven for about 35–40 minutes. Check regularly after 30 minutes to make sure it isn't burning. The baked pie should be firm to the touch but still have a slight wobble in the centre. Leave to cool completely, then cover and refrigerate overnight.

When you are ready to serve the pie, whip the cream with a handheld electric whisk in a large bowl until soft peaks form, then spread over the pie and finish with chocolate shavings.

banana cream pie

For this pie, you blind bake the pastry but the filling itself is not baked – the pie is simply filled with a custard full of banana chunks. Use very ripe bananas, be generous with the whipped cream topping and dust liberally with cinnamon. The base is covered with dulce de leche – a delicious South American soft caramel which is now easily found in supermarkets. If you're going to decorate with banana slices, remember they go brown pretty quickly, so serve immediately!

100 g dulce de leche

1 Basic Pie Crust, fully blind baked (page 96)

350 g banana (about 3 large bananas), peeled and sliced, plus extra to decorate

400 ml whipping cream

ground cinnamon, to decorate

custard

500 ml whole milk

¼ teaspoon vanilla extract

5 egg yolks

200 g caster sugar

40 g plain flour

40 g cornflour

a 23-cm pie dish, greased

Makes one 23-cm pie, to slice as desired

Preheat the oven to 175°C (160°C fan)/Gas 4.

For the custard: Put 400 ml of the milk and the vanilla extract in a medium saucepan over a medium heat and bring to the boil. Remove from the heat and leave to cool very slightly.

Put the egg yolks, sugar, flour, cornflour and remaining milk in a separate bowl and mix well to form a smooth paste.

Pour a little of the hot milk mixture into the egg mixture and stir well to combine. Pour the remaining milk mixture into the egg mixture and stir well until all the ingredients are combined.

Pour everything back into the saucepan over a low heat and bring to the boil, whisking continuously with a balloon whisk. Cook until thick, about three to five minutes. Pour the custard into a bowl, lay clingfilm directly on top (to stop a skin forming) and leave to cool completely.

Spread the dulce de leche over the base of the pie crust and arrange the slices of banana over it. Spoon the cold custard over the top. Cover and refrigerate for a couple of hours until the custard has set completely.

When you are ready to serve the pie, whip the cream with a handheld electric whisk in a large bowl until soft peaks form, then spread over the pie and decorate with more slices of banana. Finish with a generous sprinkling of cinnamon.

apple pie

You can't go wrong with a slice of warm, classic apple pie served with a scoop of vanilla ice cream. For more skilled home bakers, it's fun to decorate the top layer of pastry with cut-out leaves and other shapes. Be sure to brush the top with milk or an egg wash and sprinkle with sugar to get a beautiful, golden finish. Do also use firm, tart apples, such as Granny Smith, as they hold their shape and prevent the filling from becoming too sweet. If you use Bramley cooking apples, you'll get a mush, so stay clear.

plain flour, to dust

2 quantities Basic Pie Crust dough, unbaked (page 96)

150 g unsalted butter

3 teaspoons ground cinnamon

1.5 kg (about 12) green apples, peeled, cored and cut into medium slices

200 g caster sugar, plus extra to sprinkle

1 egg, mixed with a little milk

a 23-cm pie dish, greased

Makes one 23-cm pie, to slice as desired

Lightly dust a clean work surface with flour. Divide the dough in half. Roll out one half with a rolling pin, use to line the prepared pie dish and trim the edges with a sharp knife.

Put the butter and cinnamon in a large saucepan and heat over a medium heat until the butter has melted. Add the apples and stir until they are well coated in butter. Finally, add the sugar and stir again. Cook the apples until softened but not cooked through, then strain any remaining cooking liquid and spread them out on a tray to cool completely.

Fill the pie crust with the cold apples. Lightly dust a clean work surface with flour again. Roll out the remaining half of the dough with a rolling pin, drape over the pie dish and press down the edges, pinching to make a textured edge. Trim any excess with a sharp knife.

Make three slits in the lid of the pie to let the steam out while the pie is cooking. Make leaf shapes out of the pastry trimmings and use to decorate the pie, placing them on with some of the egg-and-milk wash. Leave the pie to rest in the refrigerator for one hour before baking.

Preheat the oven to 175°C (160°C fan)/Gas 4.

Brush the remaining egg-and-milk wash over the top of the pie with a pastry brush and sprinkle with a little extra sugar. Bake in the preheated oven for about 30–40 minutes, or until the pastry is golden brown. Serve while still warm.

blueberry pie

This is a summer favourite which should be made with lots of fresh, ripe blueberries. The cornflour thickens the filling as it cooks and keeps it firm enough to allow the pie to be sliced – once it has fully cooled down! The filling should bubble through the cuts made in the pastry lid, which is when you know the pie is ready.

plain flour, to dust

2 quantities Basic Pie Crust dough, unbaked (page 96)

100 g caster sugar

25 g cornflour

2 tablespoons freshly squeezed lemon juice

2 teaspoons finely grated lemon zest

600 g blueberries

a 23-cm pie dish, greased

Makes one 23-cm pie, to slice as desired

Lightly dust a clean work surface with flour. Divide the dough in half. Roll out one half with a rolling pin, use to line the prepared pie dish and trim the edges with a sharp knife.

Put the sugar, cornflour, lemon juice and zest and blueberries in a bowl and mix well. Fill the pie crust with the blueberry mixture. Lightly dust a clean work surface with flour again. Roll out the remaining half of the dough with a rolling pin, drape over the pie dish and press down the edges, pinching to make a textured edge. Trim any excess with a sharp knife.

Make three slits in the lid of the pie to let the steam out while the pie is cooking. Leave the pie to rest in the refrigerator for one hour before baking.

Preheat the oven to 175°C (160°C fan)/Gas 4.

Bake the pie in the preheated oven for about 40–50 minutes, or until the filling is bubbling thickly. After 30 minutes of baking, protect the edges from overcooking by covering them with foil. Leave to cool completely before serving.

brownies and bars

traditional brownie

Traditional American brownies must be chewy, chocolatey and dense. Many other brownie recipes seen outside the US are not really brownies! We don't put nuts in ours, but you can add walnuts or pecan nuts if you like. Our classic brownies are so popular in London, we sell several trays every day. For chocolate overload, you can put chocolate chips into the batter before baking.

200 g dark chocolate, roughly chopped

175 g unsalted butter

325 g caster sugar

130 g plain flour

3 eggs

icing sugar, to decorate

a 33 x 23 x 5-cm baking tray, lined with greaseproof paper

Makes about 12 portions

Preheat the oven to 170°C (155°C fan)/Gas 3½.

Put the chocolate and butter in a heatproof bowl over a saucepan of simmering water (do not let the base of the bowl touch the water). Leave until melted and smooth, stirring occasionally.

Remove from the heat. Add the sugar and stir until well incorporated. Add the flour and stir until well incorporated. Finally, stir in the eggs and mix until thick and smooth.

Spoon the mixture into the prepared baking tray and bake in the preheated oven for about 30–35 minutes, or until flaky on the top but still soft in the centre. Be careful not to overcook, otherwise the edges will become hard and crunchy. Leave to cool completely before dusting with icing sugar, to decorate.

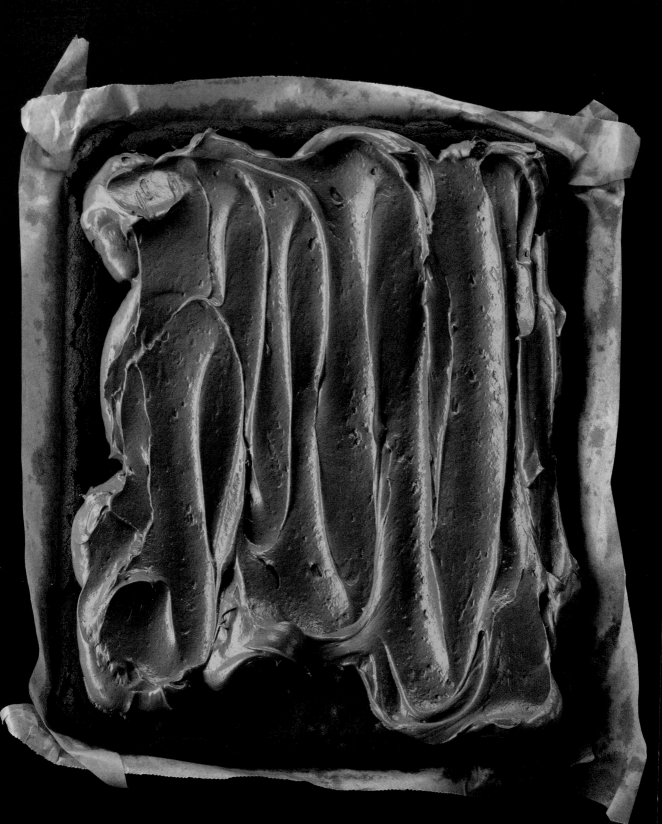

frosted brownie

Our alternative to the traditional brownie, this version is more cake-like, contains nuts, and is topped with chocolatey cream-cheese frosting.

5 eggs

500 g caster sugar

120 g plain flour, sifted

100 g cocoa powder

250 g unsalted butter, melted

30 g shelled walnuts, chopped

30 g dark chocolate, roughly chopped

frosting

200 g icing sugar, sifted

75 g unsalted butter,
at room temperature

30 g cocoa powder, sifted

150 g cream cheese, cold

*a 33 x 23 x 5-cm baking tray,
lined with greaseproof paper*

Makes 1 tray, to slice as desired

Preheat the oven to 170°C (155°C fan)/Gas 3½.

Put the eggs and sugar in a large bowl and beat with a handheld electric whisk until light and fluffy. Beat the flour and cocoa powder into the egg mixture until all the ingredients are well mixed. Pour in the melted butter and mix through. Stir in the walnuts and chocolate by hand until evenly dispersed.

Spoon the mixture into the prepared baking tray and bake in the preheated oven for about 30–35 minutes, or until the top is firm but the centre is still soft. Leave to cool completely.

For the frosting: Beat together the icing sugar, butter and cocoa powder in a freestanding electric mixer with a paddle attachment (or use a handheld electric whisk) on medium-slow speed until the mixture is well mixed and has a sandy texture. Add the cream cheese in one go and beat until it is completely incorporated. Turn the mixer up to medium-high speed. Continue beating until the frosting is light and fluffy, at least five minutes. Do not overbeat, as it can quickly become runny.

When the brownie is cold, spread the frosting over the top. Cut into pieces and serve.

raspberry cheesecake brownie

This triple-layer dessert looks irresistible when sliced: a slim layer of brownie topped with cheesecake, which are both baked together, and then covered with raspberry whipped cream. The three elements combine beautifully. You can substitute other berries in season, if you like.

brownie

200 g dark chocolate, roughly chopped

200 g unsalted butter

250 g icing sugar

3 eggs

110 g plain flour

cheesecake

400 g cream cheese

150 g icing sugar

½ teaspoon vanilla extract

2 eggs

cream topping

300 ml whipping cream

100 g icing sugar

150 g raspberries,
plus extra to decorate

*a 33 x 23 x 5-cm baking tray,
lined with greaseproof paper*

Makes 1 tray, to slice as desired

Preheat the oven to 170°C (155°C fan)/Gas 3½.

For the brownie: Put the chocolate in a heatproof bowl over a pan of simmering water (do not let the base of the bowl touch the water). Leave until melted and smooth, stirring occasionally. Put the butter and sugar in a freestanding electric mixer with a paddle attachment and beat until all the ingredients are well incorporated. Add the eggs one at a time, mixing well and scraping any unmixed ingredients from the side of the bowl with a rubber spatula after each addition. Gradually beat in the flour, mixing well after each addition, then turn the mixer up to high speed and beat for a little longer until you get a smooth mixture. Slowly pour in the melted chocolate and mix thoroughly. Pour into the prepared baking tray and smooth over with a palette knife.

For the cheesecake: Put the cream cheese, sugar and vanilla extract in a freestanding electric mixer with a paddle attachment and beat on slow speed until smooth and thick. Add one egg at a time, while still mixing. Scrape any unmixed ingredients from the side of the bowl with a rubber spatula after each addition. The mixture should be very smooth and creamy. The mixer can be turned up to a higher speed at the end to make the mix a little lighter and fluffier, but be careful not to overmix, otherwise the cheese will split. Spoon on top of the brownie and smooth over with a palette knife. Bake in the preheated oven for 30–40 minutes, or until the cheesecake is firm to the touch and light golden around the edges. The centre should still be pale. Leave to cool completely, then cover and refrigerate for two hours, or overnight if possible.

For the cream topping: Put the ingredients in a freestanding electric mixer with a whisk attachment and beat until firm but not stiff. Turn the brownie out onto a board and turn the right way up. Spread the topping evenly over the cheesecake layer and decorate with more raspberries. Cut into pieces and serve.

blondie

Here's an alternative to brownies for those who don't like the rich taste of chocolate; these blondies are made with white chocolate. Remember to let them cool completely before trying to slice and serve.

150 g white chocolate, roughly chopped

125 g unsalted butter

150 g caster sugar

2 eggs

1½ teaspoons vanilla extract

200 g plain flour

a pinch of salt

120 g shelled pecan nuts, chopped

a 33 x 23 x 5-cm baking tray, lined with greaseproof paper

Makes 1 tray, to slice as desired

Preheat the oven to 170°C (155°C fan)/Gas 3½.

Put the chocolate and butter in a heatproof bowl over a saucepan of simmering water (do not let the base of the bowl touch the water). Leave until melted and smooth, stirring occasionally.

Remove from the heat. Add the sugar and stir until well incorporated. Add the eggs and vanilla extract, stirring briskly so that you don't allow the eggs time to scramble. Don't worry if the mixture looks like it is starting to split. Add the flour, salt and pecan nuts and stir until well incorporated and the nuts are evenly dispersed.

Spoon the mixture into the prepared baking tray and bake in the preheated oven for about 25–30 minutes (but check after 20 minutes), or until golden brown and the centre is still soft. Leave to cool completely. Cut into pieces and serve.

chocolate refrigerator bars

A crunchy treat that requires no baking.

400 g unsalted butter

200 ml golden syrup

100 g cocoa powder

800 g digestive biscuits, broken into small chunks

200 g raisins

a 33 x 23 x 5-cm baking tray, lined with greaseproof paper

Makes 1 tray, to slice as desired

Put the butter, golden syrup and cocoa powder in a large saucepan over a medium heat and heat until melted and smooth, stirring occasionally.

Put the biscuit chunks and raisins in a large bowl and pour in the chocolate mixture. Mix with a wooden spoon until everything is well mixed and the biscuits and raisins are evenly dispersed.

Press this mixture into the prepared baking tray, using the back of a tablespoon to flatten and compress it. Cover with a sheet of greaseproof paper, then a tray covered in jam jars or tins to apply pressure on the cake and compress it even more. Leave to cool completely, then refrigerate for a couple of hours, or overnight if possible. Cut into pieces and serve.

muesli bars

These are packed with nuts, dried fruits and cereal. Make sure you press the mixture well into the tin and refrigerate overnight, otherwise they'll be too crumbly to slice!

320 g unsalted butter

240 ml golden syrup

250 g soft light brown sugar

250 g rolled oats

200 g desiccated coconut

125 g dried apricots, finely chopped

60 g dried dates, finely chopped

125 g cornflakes

125 g sunflower seeds

60 g dried cranberries

125 g shelled walnuts, chopped

125 g raisins

a 33 x 23 x 5-cm baking tray, lined with greaseproof paper

Makes 1 tray, to slice as desired

Put the butter, golden syrup and sugar in a large saucepan over a medium heat and heat until melted and smooth, stirring occasionally.

Put the remaining ingredients in a large bowl and stir with a wooden spoon until everything is evenly mixed. Pour in the butter mixture and mix thoroughly until everything is well mixed and the dry ingredients are evenly dispersed.

Press this mixture into the prepared baking tray, using the back of a tablespoon to flatten and compress it. Cover with a sheet of greaseproof paper, then a tray covered in jam jars or tins to apply pressure on the cake and compress it even more. Leave to cool, then refrigerate overnight. Cut into pieces and serve.

See photograph on page 126.

lemon bars

These bars are tangy and gooey. Dust with icing sugar, if you like, and make sure the bars are chilled so that they set before slicing. Try using half lemon and half lime to turn them into lemon-lime bars!

210 g caster sugar

3 eggs

100 ml freshly squeezed lemon juice

3 teaspoons finely grated lemon zest

base

290 g plain flour

70 g icing sugar

a pinch of salt

230 g unsalted butter

2 teaspoons finely grated lemon zest

a 33 x 23 x 5-cm baking tray, lined with greaseproof paper

Makes 1 tray, to slice as desired

Preheat the oven to 170°C (155°C fan)/Gas 3½.

For the base: Put the flour, sugar, salt, butter and lemon zest in a freestanding electric mixer with a paddle attachment (or use a handheld electric whisk) and beat until the mixture resembles breadcrumbs. Press the dough together with your hands, then press it evenly into the base of the prepared baking tray. Bake in the preheated oven for about 20 minutes, or until light golden. (Leave the oven on.) Leave to cool slightly.

Put the sugar, eggs and lemon juice and zest in a bowl and whisk with a balloon whisk until well mixed. Pour carefully over the baked base and return to the oven. Bake for 20 minutes, or until the edges are golden brown and the topping has set. Leave to cool completely, then cover and refrigerate overnight.

See photograph on page 127.

rocky road bars

For cute, individual servings, scoop the mixture into muffin cases before refrigerating. You can use your favourite chocolate bars instead of those specified here, just keep to the same measurements. You need to bring this back to room temperature before attempting to cut the slices.

1.4 kg milk chocolate, roughly chopped

8 regular-sized chewy, filled chocolate bars of your choice (such as Snickers and Mars), roughly chopped

100 g marshmallows

180 g chocolate-coated malt honeycomb balls (such as Maltesers)

100 g dried apricots, roughly chopped

100 g raisins

100 g cornflakes

200 g chocolate vermicelli, in two colours if possible

a 33 x 23 x 5-cm baking tray, lined with greaseproof paper

Makes 1 tray, to slice as desired

Put the milk chocolate in a heatproof bowl over a saucepan of simmering water (do not let the base of the bowl touch the water). Leave until melted and smooth, stirring occasionally.

Put the chocolate bars, marshmallows, honeycomb balls, apricots, raisins and cornflakes in a large bowl and pour in the melted chocolate. Mix with a wooden spoon until everything is well mixed and the dry ingredients are evenly dispersed.

Press this mixture into the prepared baking tray, using the back of a tablespoon to flatten and compress it. Sprinkle the chocolate vermicelli all over the top. Leave to cool completely, then cover and refrigerate for three to four hours. As it goes extremely hard, you may need to bring the rocky road back to room temperature before cutting it into slices using a warmed knife.

muffins

ham and mushroom muffins

These are a good breakfast treat. The batter is very thick and dough-like, so try spooning it into the muffin cases with an ice cream scoop.

50 g unsalted butter

½ small onion, finely chopped

80 g button mushrooms, chopped

360 g plain flour

2½ teaspoons baking powder

250 g Cheddar cheese, grated

220 ml whole milk

1 egg

80 g smoked ham, finely chopped

sea salt and freshly ground black pepper

a 12-hole muffin tray, lined with paper cases (see note on page 4)

Makes 12

Preheat the oven to 170°C (155°C fan)/Gas 3½.

Melt the butter in a saucepan over a medium heat, then fry the onion and mushrooms until cooked, about five to six minutes. Season with sea salt and pepper. Set aside.

Put the flour, baking powder and cheese in a bowl. In a separate bowl, mix the milk and egg together, then slowly pour into the flour mixture and beat with a handheld electric whisk until all the ingredients are well mixed.

Stir in the onion, mushrooms and chopped ham with a wooden spoon until evenly dispersed. The mixture will be similar to that of a dough – sticky and dense.

Divide the mixture between the paper cases until almost full and bake in the preheated oven for 30–35 minutes, or until deep golden and the sponge bounces back when touched. A skewer inserted in the centre should come out clean. Leave the muffins to cool slightly in the tray before turning out onto a wire cooling rack to cool completely.

carrot and courgette muffins

Some people are surprised to hear that courgettes can be used in muffins, but they work well and give these muffins added colour.

2 eggs

200 g soft light brown sugar

80 ml sunflower oil

260 g plain flour

2 teaspoons baking powder

2 teaspoons ground cinnamon

80 ml natural yogurt

½ teaspoon vanilla extract

120 g shelled walnuts, chopped

250 g carrots, grated

120 g courgettes, grated

a 12-hole muffin tray, lined with paper cases (see note on page 4)

Makes 12

Preheat the oven to 170°C (155°C fan)/Gas 3½.

Put the eggs, sugar and oil in an electric mixer with a paddle attachment (or use a handheld electric whisk) and beat on slow speed until well combined. In a separate bowl, sift together the flour, baking powder and cinnamon, then add to the egg mixture. Beat until everything is well incorporated.

Add the yogurt and vanilla extract and mix through until well combined. Stir in the walnuts, carrots and courgettes with a wooden spoon until evenly dispersed.

Spoon the mixture into the paper cases until two-thirds full and bake in the preheated oven for 25–30 minutes, or until deep golden and the sponge bounces back when touched. A skewer inserted in the centre should come out clean. Leave the muffins to cool slightly in the tray before turning out onto a wire cooling rack to cool completely.

spinach and cheese muffins

Here's another delicious savoury muffin that can be made using different types of hard cheese. The batter is quite thick and is easier portioned into the cases using an ice cream scoop.

30 g unsalted butter

½ small red onion, finely chopped

360 g plain flour

2½ teaspoons baking powder

1 teaspoon cayenne pepper

250 g Cheddar cheese, grated

220 ml whole milk

1 egg

130 g baby spinach leaves

*a 12-hole muffin tray,
lined with paper cases
(see note on page 4)*

Makes 12

Preheat the oven to 170°C (155°C fan)/Gas 3½.

Melt the butter in a saucepan over a medium heat, then fry the onion until cooked. Set aside.

Sift the flour, baking powder and cayenne pepper into a large bowl and stir in the cheese. In a separate bowl, mix the milk and egg together, then slowly pour into the flour mixture and beat with a handheld electric whisk until all the ingredients are well mixed.

Stir in the onion and spinach with a wooden spoon until evenly dispersed.

Spoon the mixture into the paper cases until two-thirds full and bake in the preheated oven for 30–35 minutes, or until deep golden and the sponge bounces back when touched. A skewer inserted in the centre should come out clean. Leave the muffins to cool slightly in the tray before turning out onto a wire cooling rack to cool completely.

chocolate muffins

You can vary this recipe by adding dark, milk or white chocolate chips.

2 eggs

200 g caster sugar

130 g plain flour

50 g cocoa powder

2 teaspoons baking powder

a pinch of salt

160 ml whole milk

¼ teaspoon vanilla extract

160 g unsalted butter, melted

120 g dark chocolate, roughly chopped

a 12-hole muffin tray,
lined with paper cases
(see note on page 4)

Makes 12

Preheat the oven to 170°C (155°C fan)/Gas 3½.

Put the eggs and sugar in a freestanding electric mixer with a paddle attachment (or use a handheld electric whisk) and beat until pale and well combined.

In a separate bowl, sift together the flour, cocoa powder, baking powder and salt. In another bowl, combine the milk and vanilla extract. Gradually beat these two mixtures alternately into the egg mixture little by little (scrape any unmixed ingredients from the side of the bowl with a rubber spatula). Beat until all the ingredients are well incorporated.

Stir in the melted butter with a wooden spoon until well incorporated, then stir in the chocolate until evenly dispersed.

Spoon the mixture into the paper cases until two-thirds full and bake in the preheated oven for about 30 minutes, or until the sponge bounces back when touched. A skewer inserted in the centre should come out clean. Leave the muffins to cool slightly in the tray before turning out onto a wire cooling rack to cool completely.

blueberry muffins

The classic muffin – and the perfect start to the day with a cup of strong tea. Don't worry about the blueberries sinking towards the bottom as they bake, this is perfectly normal. You can try to dust the blueberries with flour before you fold them in, but you can't fight gravity!

360 g plain flour

370 g caster sugar

1 teaspoon salt

1½ teaspoons baking powder

½ teaspoon bicarbonate of soda

375 ml buttermilk

1 egg

½ teaspoon vanilla extract

70 g unsalted butter, melted

250 g blueberries

*a 12-hole muffin tray,
lined with paper cases
(see note on page 4)*

Makes 12

Preheat the oven to 170°C (155°C fan)/Gas 3½.

Sift the flour, sugar, salt, baking powder and bicarbonate of soda into a freestanding electric mixer with a paddle attachment (or use a handheld electric whisk) and beat on slow speed.

Put the buttermilk, egg and vanilla extract into a jug and mix to combine. Slowly pour into the flour mixture and beat until all the ingredients are incorporated.

Pour in the melted butter and beat until the butter has just been incorporated, then turn the mixer up to medium speed and beat until the dough is even and smooth.

Finally, gently fold in the blueberries with a wooden spoon until evenly dispersed.

Spoon the mixture into the paper cases until two-thirds full and bake in the preheated oven for 20–25 minutes, or until golden brown and the sponge bounces back when touched. A skewer inserted in the centre should come out clean. Leave the muffins to cool slightly in the tray before turning out onto a wire cooling rack to cool completely.

banana and cinnamon muffins

Moist and sweet, nuts or chocolate chips can be added for variety. This recipe will produce muffins that spill out of their cases a bit, producing a characteristic 'muffin top'. If you don't want that, then only fill your cases three-quarters full and make a few more.

350 g plain flour

160 g caster sugar,
plus extra to sprinkle

¾ teaspoon salt

1½ teaspoons baking powder

½ teaspoon bicarbonate of soda

2 teaspoons ground cinnamon,
plus extra to sprinkle

375 ml buttermilk

1 egg

½ teaspoon vanilla extract

70 g unsalted butter, melted

400 g peeled bananas, mashed

*a 12-hole muffin tray,
lined with paper cases
(see note on page 4)*

Makes 12

Preheat the oven to 170°C (155°C fan)/Gas 3½.

Sift the flour, sugar, salt, baking powder, bicarbonate of soda and cinnamon into a large bowl and beat with a handheld electric whisk until combined.

Put the buttermilk, egg and vanilla extract in a jug and mix to combine. Slowly pour into the flour mixture and beat on slow speed until all the ingredients are incorporated.

Pour in the melted butter and beat until incorporated. Stir in the bananas with a wooden spoon until evenly dispersed.

Spoon the mixture into the paper cases until almost full and sprinkle a little extra sugar and cinnamon over the tops. Bake in the preheated oven for 30–35 minutes, or until golden brown and the sponge bounces back when touched. A skewer inserted in the centre should come out clean. Leave the muffins to cool slightly in the tray before turning out onto a wire cooling rack to cool completely.

maple and pecan muffins

Maple syrup and pecan nuts are a classic combination, with the syrup helping to make the muffins irresistibly moist and sweet. This is another recipe that will produce a 'muffin top', so if you'd prefer something neater, then fill the cases to three-quarters full and make a few extra.

350 g plain flour

160 g caster sugar

¾ teaspoon salt

1½ teaspoons baking powder

½ teaspoon bicarbonate of soda

375 ml buttermilk

1 egg

½ teaspoon vanilla extract

70 g unsalted butter, melted

175 ml maple syrup

240 g shelled pecan nuts, chopped, plus 12 pecan halves to decorate

a 12-hole muffin tray,
lined with paper cases
(see note on page 4)

Makes 12

Preheat the oven to 170°C (155°C fan)/Gas 3½.

Sift the flour, sugar, salt, baking powder and bicarbonate of soda into a large bowl and beat with a handheld electric whisk until combined.

Put the buttermilk, egg and vanilla extract in a jug and mix to combine. Slowly pour into the flour mixture and beat on slow speed until all the ingredients are incorporated.

Pour in the melted butter and beat until incorporated. Stir in 100 ml of the maple syrup and the pecan nuts with a wooden spoon until evenly dispersed.

Spoon the mixture into the paper cases until almost full and drizzle the remaining maple syrup over the tops. Finish with a pecan half in the centre of each one. Bake in the preheated oven for 20–30 minutes, or until golden brown and the sponge bounces back when touched. A skewer inserted in the centre should come out clean. Leave the muffins to cool slightly in the tray before turning out onto a wire cooling rack to cool completely.

cookies

double chocolate cookies

50 g unsalted butter

450 g dark chocolate, roughly chopped

2 eggs

170 g soft light brown sugar or light muscovado sugar

¼ teaspoon vanilla extract

85 g plain flour

½ teaspoon salt

½ teaspoon baking powder

2 baking trays, lined with greaseproof paper

Makes 12

Preheat the oven to 170°C (155°C fan)/Gas 3½.

Put the butter and half the chocolate in a heatproof bowl over a saucepan of simmering water (do not let the base of the bowl touch the water). Leave until melted and smooth.

Put the eggs, sugar and vanilla extract in a freestanding electric mixer with a paddle attachment (or use a handheld electric whisk) and beat until well mixed. Pour in the chocolate mixture, beating on slow speed until well combined.

Sift the flour, salt and baking powder into a separate bowl, then stir into the chocolate mixture in three stages, mixing well after each addition (scrape any unmixed ingredients from the side of the bowl with a rubber spatula). Finally, stir in the remaining chocolate until evenly dispersed.

Arrange six equal amounts of cookie dough on each prepared baking tray. Make sure that the cookies are spaced apart to allow for spreading while baking. Bake in the preheated oven for 10–15 minutes, checking regularly after ten minutes. They are ready when the tops start to crack and look glossy. Leave the cookies to cool slightly on the trays before transferring to a wire cooling rack to cool completely.

chocolate chip cookies

225 g unsalted butter, at room temperature

350 g soft light brown sugar

2 eggs

½ teaspoon vanilla extract

400 g plain flour

½ teaspoon salt

2½ teaspoons bicarbonate of soda

225 g dark chocolate, roughly chopped

4 baking trays, lined with greaseproof paper

Makes 24

Preheat the oven to 170°C (155°C fan)/Gas 3½.

Put the butter and sugar in a freestanding electric mixer with a paddle attachment (or use a handheld electric whisk) and cream until light and fluffy. Add the eggs one at a time, mixing well and scraping any unmixed ingredients from the side of the bowl with a rubber spatula after each addition. Turn the mixer down to slow speed and beat in the vanilla extract.

Sift the flour, salt and bicarbonate of soda and mix well until a smooth dough is formed. Stir in the chopped chocolate by hand until evenly dispersed.

Arrange six equal amounts of cookie dough on each prepared baking tray. Make sure that the cookies are spaced apart to allow for spreading while baking. Bake in the preheated oven for about ten minutes, or until golden brown around the edges and quite flat. Check them regularly to make sure they are not burning. When you are happy that they are cooked through, remove from the oven and leave to cool slightly on the trays before transferring to a wire cooling rack to cool completely. The cookies should be soft and chewy.

peanut butter cookies

These are an all-time American favourite – and whether you put chocolate chips in or not is up to you! We use crunchy peanut butter for a better texture and flavour.

225 g unsalted butter,
at room temperature

200 g caster sugar

200 g soft light brown sugar

2 eggs

½ teaspoon vanilla extract

240 g crunchy peanut butter

340 g plain flour

2½ teaspoons bicarbonate of soda

½ teaspoon salt

75 g dark chocolate, chopped
(optional)

*4 baking trays, lined with
greaseproof paper*

Makes 24

Preheat the oven to 170°C (155°C fan)/Gas 3½.

Put the butter and sugars in a freestanding electric mixer with a paddle attachment (or use a handheld electric whisk) and cream until light and fluffy. Add the eggs one at a time, mixing well and scraping any unmixed ingredients from the side of the bowl with a rubber spatula after each addition. Turn the mixer down to slow speed and beat in the vanilla extract and peanut butter.

Sift in the flour, bicarbonate of soda and salt and mix well until a smooth dough is formed. Stir in the chocolate, if using, by hand until evenly dispersed.

Arrange six equal amounts of cookie dough on each prepared baking tray. Make sure that the cookies are spaced apart to allow for spreading while baking. Bake in the preheated oven for about ten minutes, or until golden brown around the edges and quite flat. Check them regularly to make sure they are not burning. When you are happy that they are cooked through, remove from the oven and leave to cool slightly on the trays before transferring to a wire cooling rack to cool completely. The cookies should be soft and chewy.

white chocolate and pecan nut cookies

This is a flavour combination that works very well to create a more sophisticated cookie. Dark or milk chocolate can be substituted if you don't like white chocolate.

250 g unsalted butter,
at room temperature

100 g caster sugar

200 g soft light brown sugar

2 eggs

½ teaspoon vanilla extract

400 g plain flour

½ teaspoon salt

¼ teaspoon baking powder

100 g white chocolate, chopped

100 g shelled pecan nuts, chopped

4 baking trays, lined with greaseproof paper

Makes 20

Put the butter and sugars in a freestanding electric mixer with a paddle attachment (or use a handheld electric whisk) and cream until light and fluffy. Add the eggs one at a time, mixing well and scraping any unmixed ingredients from the side of the bowl with a rubber spatula after each addition. Turn the mixer down to slow speed and beat in the vanilla extract.

Sift in the flour, salt and baking powder and mix well until a smooth dough is formed. Stir in the chocolate and pecan nuts by hand until evenly dispersed.

Divide the dough in half and shape each half into two equal rolls measuring 20 cm in length. Wrap the rolls in clingfilm and put them in the freezer to set completely for a couple of hours.

Preheat the oven to 170°C (155°C fan)/Gas 3½.

Remove the clingfilm and cut the dough into discs about 2 cm thick. Arrange the cookies on the prepared baking trays. Make sure that the cookies are spaced apart to allow for spreading while baking. Bake in the preheated oven for 10–15 minutes, or until golden brown around the edges and quite flat. Check them regularly to make sure they are not burning. When you are happy that they are cooked through, remove from the oven and leave to cool slightly on the trays before transferring to a wire cooling rack to cool completely. The cookies should be soft and chewy.

oat and raisin cookies

Here's a lovely, cinnamony cookie made with rolled oats.

270 g unsalted butter,
at room temperature

160 g caster sugar

160 g soft dark brown sugar

2 eggs

¼ teaspoon vanilla extract

380 g plain flour

1 teaspoon salt

1 teaspoon bicarbonate of soda

½ teaspoon ground cinnamon

110 g rolled oats

220 g raisins

*4 baking trays, lined with
greaseproof paper*

Makes 20

Preheat the oven to 170°C (155°C fan)/Gas 3½.

Put the butter and sugars in a freestanding electric mixer with
a paddle attachment (or use a handheld electric whisk) and
cream until light and fluffy. Add the eggs one at a time, mixing
well and scraping any unmixed ingredients from the side of the
bowl with a rubber spatula after each addition. Turn the mixer
down to slow speed and beat in the vanilla extract.

Sift together the flour, salt, bicarbonate of soda and cinnamon
in a separate bowl, add the oats and mix well. Add to the
butter mixture and beat until well mixed. Stir in the raisins with a
wooden spoon until evenly dispersed.

Arrange equal amounts of cookie dough on the prepared
baking trays. Make sure that the cookies are spaced apart to
allow for spreading while baking. Bake in the preheated oven
for about 15–18 minutes, or until golden brown and firm. Check
them regularly to make sure they are not burning. When you
are happy that they are cooked through, remove from the oven
and leave to cool slightly on the trays before transferring to a
wire cooling rack to cool completely.

sugar cookies

This recipe forms the base for a perfect cut-out cookie to suit any occasion! Roll out the dough and use shaped cookie cutters to make your own festive cookies.

200 g unsalted butter,
at room temperature

280 g caster sugar

¼ teaspoon vanilla extract

1 egg

400 g plain flour, plus extra to dust

a pinch of salt

½ teaspoon cream of tartar

Royal Icing (page 156)

2–3 tablespoons water

shaped biscuit cutters

*4 baking trays, lined with
greaseproof paper*

Makes about 40

Preheat the oven to 170°C (155°C fan)/Gas 3½.

Put the butter, sugar and vanilla extract in a freestanding electric mixer with a paddle attachment (or use a handheld electric whisk) and cream until light and fluffy. Add the egg and mix well, scraping any unmixed ingredients from the side of the bowl with a rubber spatula.

Add the flour, salt and cream of tartar and mix well, but don't overmix. The dough should be light, soft and easy to handle.

Lightly dust a clean work surface with flour and roll out the dough with a rolling pin. Cut out shapes with your choice of biscuit cutters. Arrange the cookies on the prepared baking trays and bake in the preheated oven for about ten minutes. Check them regularly to make sure they are not burning. The cookies should be very light golden on the outer edges and paler in the centre. When you are happy that they are cooked through, remove from the oven and leave to cool slightly on the trays before transferring to a wire cooling rack to cool completely. Decorate with Royal Icing, adding the water to achieve a spreadable consistency.

gingerbread men

You don't have to use a gingerbread man cutter with this recipe, but it's so much fun to decorate each one individually. Leaving the dough to rest overnight makes the cookies taste better and the dough easier to handle.

400 g plain flour, plus extra to dust

¾ teaspoon bicarbonate of soda

2 teaspoons ground ginger

2 teaspoons ground cinnamon

½ teaspoon ground allspice

¼ teaspoon ground nutmeg

½ teaspoon salt

180 g unsalted butter,
at room temperature

125 g soft dark brown sugar
or dark muscovado sugar

1 egg

125 g black treacle

royal icing

1 egg white

1 teaspoon freshly squeezed
lemon juice

1 tablespoon water

310 g icing sugar, sifted

food colouring, optional

gingerbread biscuit cutters

*a baking tray, lined with
greaseproof paper*

Makes about 24

Sift together the flour, bicarbonate of soda, ginger, cinnamon, allspice, nutmeg and salt in a large bowl and set aside.

Put the butter and sugar in a freestanding electric mixer with a paddle attachment (or use a handheld electric whisk) and cream on slow speed until light and fluffy. Turn the mixer up to medium speed and beat in the egg and treacle, scraping any unmixed ingredients from the side of the bowl with a rubber spatula.

Turn the mixer back down to slow speed and slowly add the flour mixture a couple of tablespoons at a time, stopping often to scrape any unmixed ingredients from the side of the bowl with a rubber spatula. Once an even dough has formed, take it out of the mixer, divide into three and wrap each piece in clingfilm. Leave to rest overnight in the fridge.

When you are ready to bake the cookies, preheat the oven to 170°C (155°C fan)/Gas 3½.

Take the dough out of the fridge and leave to soften for about ten minutes. Lightly dust a clean work surface with flour and roll out the dough to a thickness of about 4 mm with a rolling pin. Cut out shapes with the biscuit cutters. Arrange the cookies on the prepared baking trays and bake in the preheated oven for about 10–15 minutes. Leave the cookies to cool slightly on the trays before transferring to a wire cooling rack to cool completely.

For the royal icing: Beat the egg white, lemon juice and water together in a freestanding electric mixer with a whisk attachment (or use a handheld electric whisk). Gradually start adding the icing sugar, mixing well after each addition to ensure all sugar is incorporated. Whisk until you get stiff peaks, about five minutes. If the icing is too runny, add a little more sugar. Stir in a couple of drops of food colouring, if using, and decorate the cookies using a piping bag.

index

author's acknowledgements

With thanks to all The Hummingbird Bakery chefs who have worked on the recipes in this book over the years, including: Simone Tasker, Joanne Adams, Jhanet Thyssen and Barbara Bachota. A very special thank you to Heath MacIntyre for her very hard and excellent work on the original edition of this book and to Rachel Wood for re-testing the revised and new recipes. Thanks to the original team who designed, photographed, edited and styled this classic: Steve Painter, Peter Cassidy, Bridget Sargeson and Céline Hughes; and to Kate Whitaker, Annie Rigg and Olivia Wardle for the photography and styling of the new recipe additions. Huge thanks to my agent Zoë Waldie and to Alison Starling and all the team at Octopus Publishing for making this new edition happen. Finally, a big thank you to all the staff, past and present, who have made The Hummingbird Bakery such a success.

publisher's acknowledgements

Thanks to the following for the kind loan of props for this book:

Jane Wicks, Kitchenalia
'Country Ways'
Strand Quay
Rye
East Sussex
TN31 7DB